The Bonnie & Camille Quilt Bee

By Bonnie Olaveson of Cotton Way
and Camille Roskelley of Thimble Blossoms

The Bonnie & Camille Quilt Bee

Authors and Designers - Bonnie Olaveson and Camille Roskelley

Editor in Chief - Kimberly Jolly

Art Director - Sarah Price

Editorial Director - Jocelyn Ueng

Copy Editors - Nova Birchfield, Cheryl Cohorn, Karen Hardy, Peach Lambert and Denise Rudolph

Photographers - Camille Roskelley, Bonnie Olaveson, Sarah Price and Shelby Peck

Published by:
Fat Quarter Shop®
2899 Business Park Drive
Buda, TX 78610

www.FatQuarterShop.com · www.ItsSewEmma.com

ISBN: 978-1-7339608-9-2

Foreword

If you're wondering how it came to be that I am writing this, it started with a parade. But I'll get to that in a moment.

There has been much written about the importance of connections in our lives, how they bring us joy, purpose and meaning. Our first connections are with family, then with playmates and classmates who become friends. We bond over something we share - a heritage, an experience or a love for cutting pretty fabric into little pieces.

I'm sure that many of you are like me in that most of my dearest friends are quilters. That is how I met Camille, and then Bonnie. Even though we'd both been in the quilt industry for many years, I only knew Bonnie through her patterns. She lived in Idaho with her sweet husband, and she was a mom to five kids. I was single, lived in Arizona and had a dog, Rosie.

Camille? We met online. I loved her patterns and she wrote a terrific blog about her young family. She made one of my patterns, and no, I don't hold it against her that her quilt was prettier than mine. We bonded over the quilts we made and the fabric we loved.

Then one day, we decided to blog about the first quilt we'd each made. We encouraged others to do the same. Within a few days, hundreds of quilters had shared their first quilts with others who would become new quilting friends.

Along the way it was a parade of wonky seams, chopped off points and lumps and bumps of unknown origin. There was even a famous quilter who kept trying to throw away her first quilt, only to have it rescued by her husband. We shared our stories. We made connections. We are quilters.

- Carrie Nelson

Table of Contents

Introduction: How Quilting Bees Came to Be

Quilting has been around forever, it seems. The earliest quilts date all the way back to early Egyptians, although quilting became much more widespread in 1800s America. Many American settlers, including our pioneer ancestors, made quilts to keep their families warm out of clothing that could no longer be patched and reused. At some point, these clever women realized that if they got together with friends and neighbors and traded these precious scraps, they could create more variety in their quilts. These patchwork quilts would become quilting as we know it and were the beginning of the quilting bee.

A "bee" is another word for a party or social gathering where people work together to accomplish a specific project. Quilting bees quickly gained popularity and became a regular occurrence in many households and communities. Quiltmaking was born out of necessity, but also out of pleasure. Quilting bees became an opportunity for women to gather and socialize while using their creativity to provide for their loved ones.

Quilting Bee, circa 1910s

Friends and neighbors often lived quite a distance away, so these quilting bees were certainly something these women looked forward to. During the long winters, they worked diligently on quilt blocks, and once the weather warmed up, they would gather in a home (or outside when the weather was nice) to hand quilt the quilts. Over the quilting frame, women would swap recipes, give advice on raising children and connect over shared life experiences. Quilting bees were great places to learn new skills and share blocks, but were primarily based around hand quilting special quilts that marked important life events.

Many of the quilts made at these quilting bees are still around today, and the quilting bee tradition lives on as well. Though it may look a little different today, modern quilting bees have taken on other forms. They may look like quilt retreats, local quilt guilds, sewing with friends or family members, participating in an online sew along or even swapping blocks around the world with other quilters. And that's just the beginning.

Although it is definitely our favorite way to spend the day, quilting can get a little lonely at times. Reaching out beyond our sewing machines and connecting with other quilters can bring so much joy to this wonderful quilting world of ours. In this book, we will highlight some of our favorite ways to connect with our fellow quilting friends near and far as we share a love of quiltmaking.

While we love the beautiful quilts, this amazing community is what we enjoy most about quilting. We hope that this book will inspire you to be a part of it. Thank you so much for being part of our quilting bee and for all the encouragement you've given us all these years. We love sewing with you.

— Bonnie & Camille

You Have My Heart Quilt

Pieced by Bonnie Olaveson, Bailey Berrett, Sydney Berrett, Anni Berrett & Olivia Boyce
Quilted by Susan Hansen
Fabric from various Bonnie & Camille collections for Moda Fabrics

You Have My Heart Quilt

Sewing with my grandchildren is one of my very favorite things to do. I started out teaching them one by one how to use a sewing machine, and now we can team up on a project together while everyone works on their own blocks. Although this sewing day was with my granddaughters, I should also mention that several of my grandsons are also excellent sewers, and my oldest grandson has a knack for sewing neckties that his brothers and cousins love. I feel so lucky every time I get to sew with one of them.

For this particular sewing day, I had some of my granddaughters sign their blocks to remember them at this age and treasure this special day. A nod to the friendship quilts from so long ago, the wall quilt we made together is one I will hang in my home and cherish.

You don't need grandchildren of your own to share your quilting knowledge. Reach out to your friends and neighbors to see if any children near you might like to learn to sew. Check with your church or community to see if there is a need for sewing teachers. Passing a love of sewing and quilting to the next generation is such a wonderful thing and will make your heart so happy!

— Bonnie

You Have My Heart Quilt

Cutting Instructions:

Background & Borders - 4 ⅓ yards

3 - 12 ½" x WOF strips, subcut into:	
4 - 8 ½" x 12 ½" rectangles	A
13 - 4 ½" x 12 ½" rectangles	B
6 - 6 ½" x WOF strips, subcut into:	
36 - 6 ½" squares	C
5 - 2 ½" x WOF strips, subcut into:	
72 - 2 ½" squares	D
10 - 2 ½" x WOF strips, sew end to end and subcut into:	
6 - 2 ½" x 60 ½" strips	E
5 - 6 ½" x WOF strips, sew end to end and subcut into:	
2 - 6 ½" x 72 ½" strips	F

Blocks -
One Jelly Roll (36 - 2 ½" x WOF strips)

From 30 - 2 ½" x WOF strips cut:	
3 - 2 ½" x 12 ½" rectangles (90 total)	G
From 6 - 2 ½" x WOF strips cut:	
6 - 2 ½" x 6 ½" rectangles (36 total)	H

Binding - ¾ yard

8 - 2 ½" x WOF strips	I

Backing - 4 ⅝ yards

Another Idea:
Scrappy Reds and Pinks on Gray

You Have My Heart Blocks:

Each You Have My Heart Block uses six color coordinating scrappy prints.

Draw a diagonal line on the wrong side of the Fabric D squares.

With right sides facing, layer a Fabric D square on the left end of a Fabric H rectangle.

Stitch on the drawn line and trim ¼" away from the seam.

Repeat on the right end.

Top Heart Unit should measure 2 ½" x 6 ½".

Make thirty-six.

Assemble Unit using coordinating fabric. Press open. Heart Unit should measure 12 ½" x 12 ½".

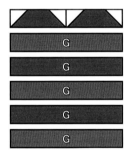 

Make eighteen.

...aw a diagonal line on the wrong side of the Fabric C
...uares.

...ith right sides facing, layer a Fabric C square on the
...ottom left corner of a Heart Unit.

...itch on the drawn line and trim ¼" away from the
...am.

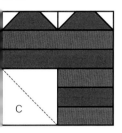 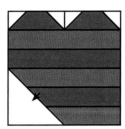

...epeat on the bottom right corner.

...u Have My Heart Block should measure
...½" x 12 ½".

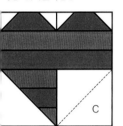 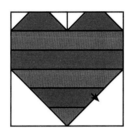

...ake eighteen.

You Have My Heart Quilt

Quilt Assembly:

Assemble Quilt Center. Press toward the background.

Quilt Center should measure 60 ½" x 68 ½".

Attach side borders using the remaining Fabric E strips.

Attach top and bottom borders using the Fabric F strips.

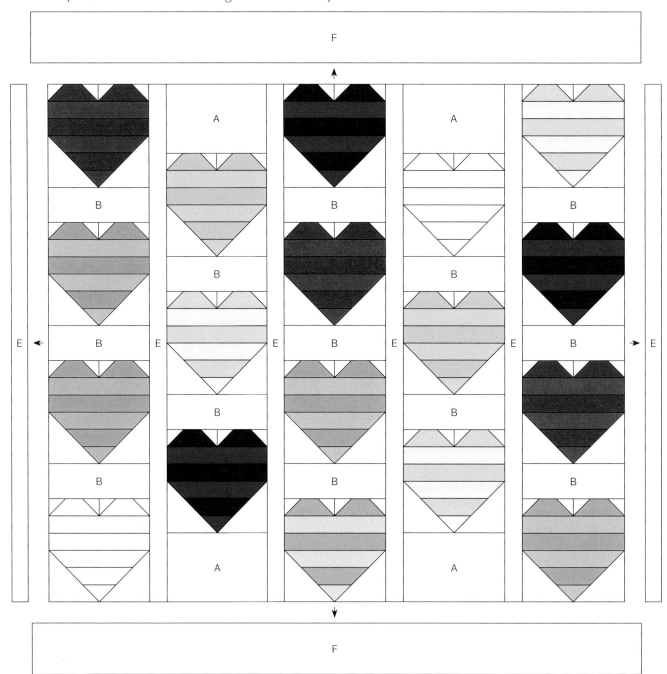

Finishing:

Piece the Fabric I strips end to end for binding.

Quilt and bind as desired.

Signature Blocks

For signature blocks, make sure you use an ultra-fine permanent marker that won't bleed. Practice on a test scrap before signing the actual blocks, because fabric is a little trickier to write on than paper. This works well for quilt labels too.

Legacy Quilt

Pieced by Camille Roskelley, Bonnie Olaveson & Phyllis Beesley Moss
Quilted by Abby Latimer
Fabric from Early Bird by Bonnie & Camille for Moda Fabrics

Legacy Quilt

In the 1960s, my great-grandma Sarah made and quilted a quilt for each of her 11 children and was photographed for her local newspaper. Her mother taught her to sew as a young girl, and when she had children of her own, she taught them how to sew too. One of her girls, my grandma, has made countless quilts in her 93 years of life and has passed on a love of quilting to many of her 10 children. She taught my mom how to piece, quilt and bind, and she in turn taught me those very same things. A legacy that goes all the way back to our pioneer heritage, quilting binds the women of our family together in a unique way. Our mutual love of cutting up little pieces of fabric and sewing them together made this special sewing day and this quilt such a wonderful one.

Camille

Legacy Quilt

Cutting Instructions:

Background - 4 ⅛ yards	
5 - 5" x WOF strips, subcut into:	
36 - 5" squares	A
9 - 4 ½" x WOF strips, subcut into:	
72 - 4 ½" squares	B
30 - 2 ½" x WOF strips, subcut into:	
72 - 2 ½" x 6 ½" rectangles	C
72 - 2 ½" x 4 ½" rectangles	D
144 - 2 ½" squares	E

Blocks - One Layer Cake (36 - 10" squares)	
From each 10" square cut:	
1 - 5" square (36 total)	F
6 - 2 ½" squares (216 total)	G
6 - 2 ½" squares (216 total)	H

Binding - ¾ yard	
8 - 2 ½" x WOF strips	I

Backing - 4 ⅝ yards	

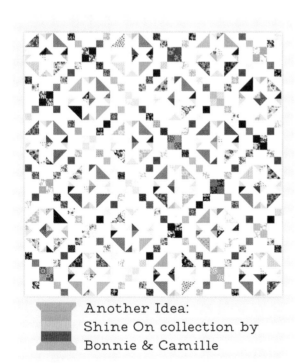

Another Idea:
Shine On collection by
Bonnie & Camille

Criss Cross Blocks:

Fabric placement is intended to be scrappy.

Assemble Unit using matching fabric.
Center Four Patch Unit should measure 4 ½" x 4 ½".

Make eighteen.

Assemble Unit.
Outer Four Patch Unit should measure 4 ½" x 4 ½".

Make seventy-two.

Assemble Block. Press open.
Criss Cross Block should measure 12 ½" x 12 ½".

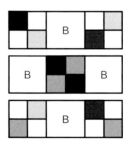 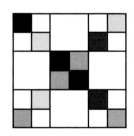

Make eighteen.

eighborhood Blocks:

bric placement is intended to be scrappy.

---

aw a diagonal line on the wrong side of the Fabric A
uares.

th right sides facing, layer a Fabric A square with a
bric F square.

itch ¼" from each side of the drawn line.

it apart on the marked line.

IM Half Square Triangle Unit to measure
½" x 4 ½".

ake seventy-two.

---

aw a diagonal line on the wrong side of the Fabric H
uares.

th right sides facing, layer a Fabric H square on the
p end of a Fabric D rectangle.

itch on the drawn line and trim ¼" away from the
am.

ght Neighborhood Unit should measure 2 ½" x 4 ½".

ake seventy-two.

With right sides facing, layer a Fabric H square on the
left end of a Fabric C rectangle.

Stitch on the drawn line and trim ¼" away from the
seam.

Repeat on the right end with different fabric.

Bottom Neighborhood Unit should measure
2 ½" x 6 ½".

Make seventy-two.

Assemble Unit. Press open.

Neighborhood Unit should measure 6 ½" x 6 ½".

Make seventy-two.

Assemble Block. Press open.

Neighborhood Block should measure 12 ½" x 12 ½".

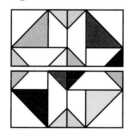 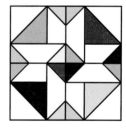

Make eighteen.

Legacy Quilt

Quilt Assembly:

Assemble Quilt Center. Press rows open.

Quilt Center should measure 72 ½" x 72 ½".

Finishing:

Piece the Fabric I strips end to end for binding.

Quilt and bind as desired.

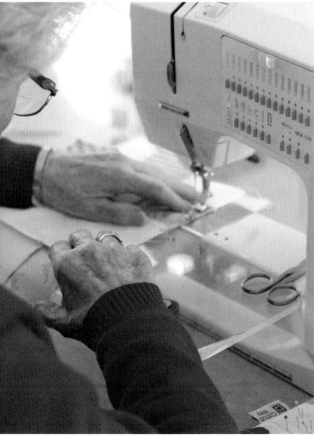

Rainbow Baby Quilt

Pieced by Camille Roskelley
Quilted by Abby Latimer
Fabric from various Bonnie & Camille collections for Moda Fabrics

Rainbow Baby Quilt

One of my earliest memories is playing with my cousins under a quilt frame set up in my grandma's front room while my grandma, her sisters and my aunts worked on a quilt. As I listened to them talk, I wondered if I, too, would be a quilter someday. Although I made a few quilts with my mom when I was young, it wasn't until I was making a baby quilt for my second son that I fell in love with quilting. With two children under two, it gave me a task that, unlike the piles of laundry and loads of dishes, stayed done. Once I started, I couldn't stop. It felt like it was a part of me that had always been there. I still love making baby quilts and have made many of them over the years for my family and friends. This little rainbow one is especially dear to my heart, a reminder of a sweet baby girl.

— Camille

The Bonnie & Camille 19 Quilt Bee

Rainbow Baby Quilt

Cutting Instructions:

Background & Borders - 1 ⅞ yards	
23 - 2" x WOF strips, subcut into:	
84 - 2" x 3 ½" rectangles	A
84 - 2" squares	B
168 - 2" squares	C
5 - 2 ½" x WOF strips, sew end to end and subcut into:	
2 - 2 ½" x 42 ½" strips	D
2 - 2 ½" x 40 ½" strips	E

Blocks - Scraps in Red, Pink, Orange, Yellow, Green, Aqua and Navy (7 colors - 12 prints of each)	
From 3 prints of each color cut:	
8 - 2" squares (168 total)	F
From 3 prints of each color cut:	
4 - 2" x 3 ½" rectangles (84 total)	G
4 - 2" squares (84 total)	H
From 6 prints of each color cut:	
1 - 3 ½" square (42 total)	I

Binding - ½ yard	
5 - 2 ½" x WOF strips	J

| Backing - 2 ⅞ yards | |

Evening Star Blocks:

Each Evening Star Block uses two color coordinating scrappy prints.

Draw a diagonal line on the wrong side of the Fabric C squares.

With right sides facing, layer a Fabric C square on one end of a Fabric G rectangle.

Stitch on the drawn line and trim ¼" away from the seam.

Repeat on the opposite end.

Evening Star Flying Geese Unit should measure 2" x 3 ½".

Make eighty-four.

Assemble Block using color coordinating fabric. Press open.

Evening Star Block should measure 6 ½" x 6 ½".

Make three from each color.
Make twenty-one total.

Another Idea:
Navy, Aqua, Green and
Gray on White

ight Point Star Blocks:

ch Eight Point Star Block uses two color
ordinating scrappy prints.

---

aw a diagonal line on the wrong side of the Fabric F
uares.

th right sides facing, layer a Fabric F square on one
d of a Fabric A rectangle.

tch on the drawn line and trim ¼" away from the
am.

peat on the opposite end with matching fabric.

ght Point Star Flying Geese Unit should measure
x 3 ½".

ke eighty-four.

---

semble Block using color coordinating fabric. Press
en.

ght Point Star Block should measure 6 ½" x 6 ½".

ke three from each color.
ke twenty-one total.

Quilt Assembly:

Assemble Quilt Center. Pay close attention to block
placement. Each row uses the same color of fabric.
Press open.

Quilt Center should measure 36 ½" x 42 ½".

Attach side borders using the Fabric D strips.

Attach top and bottom borders using the Fabric E
strips.

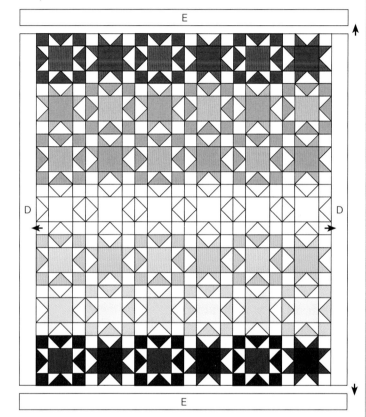

Finishing:

Piece the Fabric J strips end to end for binding.

Quilt and bind as desired.

Starburst Quilt

Pieced by Bonnie Olaveson and Danette Miller
Quilted by Susan Hansen
Fabric from various Bonnie & Camille collections for Moda Fabrics

Starburst Quilt

It's been over 20 years since my friend and neighbor, Danette, and I started having quilt day. Between us, we had 10 kids still at home and a lot going on every day, but we realized that if we made time to get together and sew, we were always happy we did. Our quilt day is simple, just a few hours of sewing, catching up and a quick trip into town to get some lunch. Through two decades, we have made too many quilts together to count and have helped each other through life's ups and downs, including raising teenagers, fighting cancer and losing loved ones. Our friendship has grown, and so have all of our children and now grandchildren. Our quilt day has done more than make quilts, it has enriched both of our lives in a way we could never have imagined that very first quilt day.

— *Bonnie*

Starburst Quilt

Cutting Instructions:

Background & Borders - 4 ⅔ yards	
13 - 3 ½" x WOF strips, subcut into:	
26 - 3 ½" x 9 ½" rectangles	A
52 - 3 ½" squares	B
7 - 2 ½" x WOF strips, subcut into:	
104 - 2 ½" squares	C
26 - 2" x WOF strips, subcut into:	
208 - 2" x 5" rectangles	D
14 - 1 ½" x WOF strips, subcut into:	
40 - 1 ½" x 12 ½" rectangles	E
8 - 3" x WOF strips, sew end to end and subcut into:	
2 - 3" x 64 ½" strips	F
2 - 3" x 69 ½" strips	G

Blocks - Thirteen Fat Quarters (13 - 18" x 21" rectangles)	
From each fat quarter cut:	
8 - 2 ½" squares (104 total)	H
24 - 2" squares (312 total)	I
16 - 2" squares (208 total)	J

Cornerstones - One 10" square	
From the 10" square cut:	
16 - 1 ½" squares	K

Binding - ¾ yard	
8 - 2 ½" x WOF strips	L

| Backing - 4 ½ yards | |

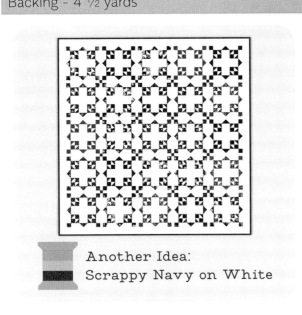

Another Idea:
Scrappy Navy on White

Starburst Blocks:

Each fat quarter makes two Starburst Blocks.

Draw a diagonal line on the wrong side of the Fabric C squares.

With right sides facing, layer a Fabric C square with a Fabric H square.

Stitch ¼" from each side of the drawn line.

Cut apart on the marked line.

TRIM Half Square Triangle Unit to measure 2" x 2".

Make two hundred eight.

Assemble Unit using matching fabric. Press open.
Partial Inner Unit should measure 3 ½" x 3 ½".

Make one hundred four.

Assemble Unit using matching fabric.
Inner Unit should measure 9 ½" x 9 ½".

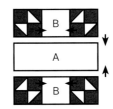 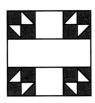

Make twenty-six.

raw a diagonal line on the wrong side of the Fabric J
quares.

ith right sides facing, layer a Fabric J square on the
ght end of a Fabric D rectangle.

titch on the drawn line and trim ¼" away from the
eam.

eft Unit should measure 2" x 5".

ake one hundred four.

ith right sides facing, layer a Fabric J square on the
ft end of a Fabric D rectangle.

titch on the drawn line and trim ¼" away from the
eam.

ght Unit should measure 2" x 5".

ake one hundred four.

ssemble Unit using matching fabric. Press open.
uter Unit should measure 2" x 9 ½".

ake one hundred four.

ssemble Block using matching fabric. Press open.
tarburst Block should measure 12 ½" x 12 ½".

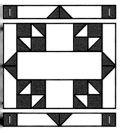 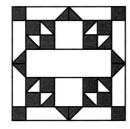

ake twenty-six.
ou will not use one Starburst Block.

Starburst Quilt

Quilt Assembly:

Assemble Quilt Center using Fabric E rectangles for sashing and Fabric K squares for cornerstones. Press toward th[e] background.

Quilt Center should measure 64 ½" x 64 ½".

Attach side borders using the Fabric F strips.

Attach top and bottom borders using the Fabric G strips.

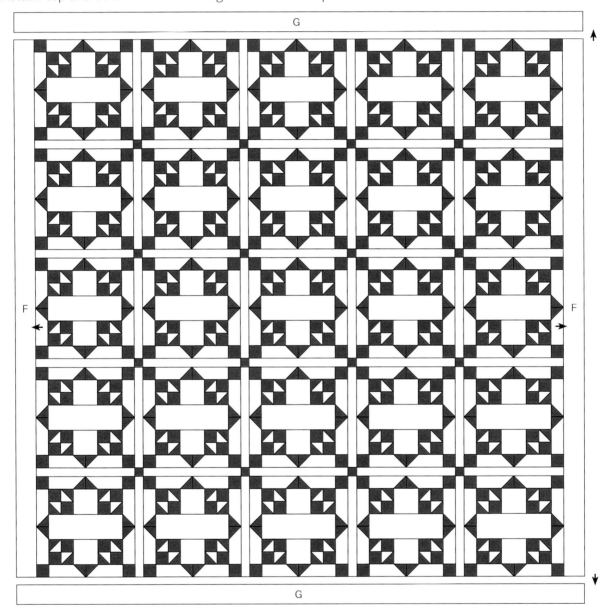

Finishing:

Piece the Fabric L strips end to end for binding.

Quilt and bind as desired.

Weekender Quilt

Pieced by Camille Roskelley, Dana Gonsalves, Megan Hilvers, Samantha Olsen, Nicole Christoffersen, Abby Latimer & Julia Davis / Quilted by Abby Latimer
Fabric from various Bonnie & Camille collections for Moda Fabrics

Weekender Quilt

A few years ago at a snowy quilt retreat where I was teaching in the Utah mountains, a group of quilters sat together and sewed for a weekend. We didn't know each other when we got there, but by the time we left, we were fast friends with a promise to get together again soon. That was the beginning of our little retreat group. We live in California, Utah, Nevada and Colorado, so it is often tricky to coordinate a weekend to get together, but when we see each other, it's like we never missed a beat. We've made a few projects together over the years and had such a great time getting together to work on this quilt. The moral of the story? The next time you go to a quilting retreat, make sure to get to know the people around you. They could become lifelong friends.

— *Camille*

Weekender Quilt

Cutting Instructions:

Background & Borders - 3 ¾ yards	
55 - 2" x WOF strips, subcut into:	
21 - 2" x 21" strips	A
30 - 2" x 21" strips	B
80 - 2" x 8" rectangles	C
80 - 2" x 5" rectangles	D
42 - 2" squares	E
8 - 2" x WOF strips, sew end to end and subcut into:	
2 - 2" x 68" strips	F
2 - 2" x 71" strips	G

Blocks - One Fat Eighth Bundle (35 - 9" x 21" rectangles)	
From 21 - 9" x 21" rectangles cut:	
2 - 2" x 21" strips (42 total)	H
1 - 2" x 21" strip (21 total)	I
1 - 2" x 21" strip (21 total)	J
From 10 - 9" x 21" rectangles cut:	
3 - 2" x 21" strips (30 total)	K
1 - 2" x 21" strip (10 total)	L1
From 4 - 9" x 21" rectangles cut:	
3 - 2" x 21" strips (12 total)	L2

Binding - ¾ yard	
8 - 2 ½" x WOF strips	M

Backing - 4 ½ yards	

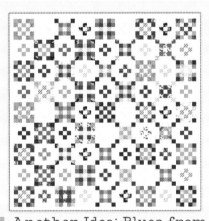

Another Idea: Blues from At Home collection by Bonnie & Camille

Plaid Blocks:

Each Plaid Block uses four different prints.

Assemble one Fabric I strip and one coordinating Fabric H strip. Use each Fabric H print once. Press open.

Strip Set One should measure 3 ½" x 21".

Make twenty-one.

Subcut each Strip Set One into eight 2" x 3 ½" rectangles.

Two Patch Unit One should measure 2" x 3 ½".

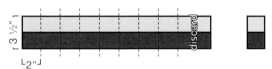

Make one hundred sixty-eight.

Assemble one Fabric H strip and one coordinating Fabric L strip. Press open.

Strip Set Two should measure 3 ½" x 21".

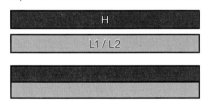

Make twenty-one.
You will not use one Fabric L strip.

Subcut each Strip Set Two into eight 2" x 3 ½" rectangles.

Two Patch Unit Two should measure 2" x 3 ½".

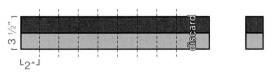

Make one hundred sixty-eight.

ssemble Unit using matching Fabric H prints. Press
pen.

our Patch Unit should measure 3 ½" x 3 ½".

lake one hundred sixty-eight.

ssemble one Fabric A strip and one Fabric J strip.
ress open.

trip Set Three should measure 3 ½" x 21".

lake twenty-one.

ubcut each Strip Set Three into eight 2" x 3 ½"
ectangles.

wo Patch Unit Three should measure 2" x 3 ½".

lake one hundred sixty-eight.

ssemble Block using coordinating fabric. Press open.

laid Block should measure 8" x 8".

ake forty-two.
ou will not use one Plaid Block.

Nine Patch Blocks:

Assemble two matching Fabric K strips and one
Fabric B strip. Press open.

Strip Set Four should measure 5" x 21".

Make ten.

Subcut each Strip Set Four into four 2" x 5" rectangles.

Inner Three Patch Unit should measure 2" x 5".

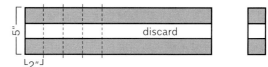

Make forty.

Assemble two Fabric B strips and one Fabric K strip.
Press open.

Strip Set Five should measure 5" x 21".

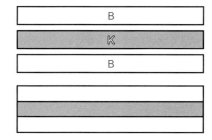

Make ten.

Subcut each Strip Set Five into eight 2" x 5" rectangles.

Outer Three Patch Unit should measure 2" x 5".

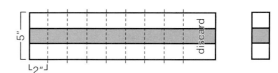

Make eighty.

Weekender Quilt

Assemble Unit using matching fabric. Press open.

Nine Patch Unit should measure 5" x 5".

Make forty.

Assemble Block. Press open.

Nine Patch Block should measure 8" x 8".

Make forty.

Quilt Assembly:

Assemble Quilt Center. Press open.

Quilt Center should measure 68" x 68".

Attach side borders using the Fabric F strips.

Attach top and bottom borders using the Fabric G strips.

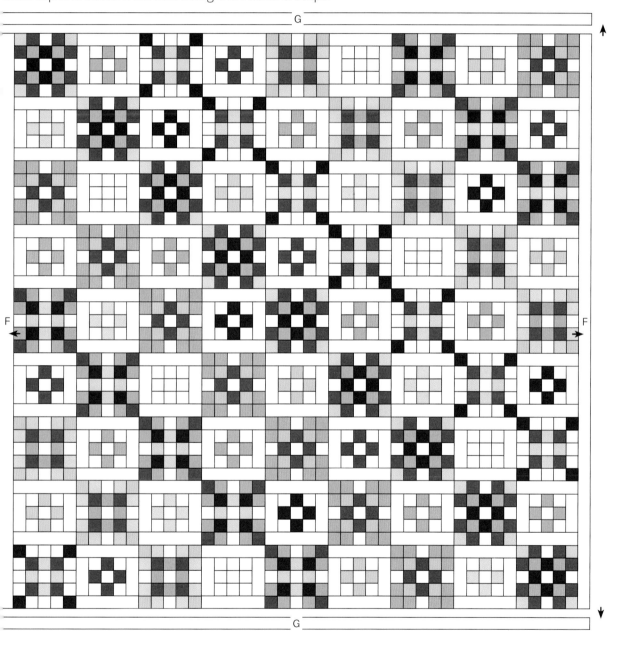

Finishing:

Piece the Fabric M strips end to end for binding.

Quilt and bind as desired.

Wish Table Runner

Pieced by Bonnie Olaveson
Quilted by Susan Hansen
Fabric from Smitten by Bonnie & Camille for Moda Fabrics

Wish Table Runner

A table runner is one of my favorite things to make and I wish I knew how many I've made over the years. Too many to count! They come together quickly, make wonderful gifts and are the perfect way to brighten a kitchen table. This one is made out of Layer Cake squares and has a pieced backing as well, making it reversible. Whip one up in an afternoon for you or for someone you love.

— *Bonnie*

Wish Table Runner

Cutting Instructions:

Background & Inner Borders - 1 ¼ yards

3 - 4 ⅞" x WOF strips, subcut into: 18 - 4 ⅞" squares	A
2 - 4 ½" x WOF strips, subcut into: 12 - 4 ½" squares	B
2 - 2 ⅞" x WOF strips, subcut into: 24 - 2 ⅞" squares	C
2 - 1 ½" x WOF strips, subcut into: 4 - 1 ½" x 16 ½" strips	D
3 - 1 ½" x WOF strips, sew end to end and subcut into: 2 - 1 ½" x 52 ½" strips	E

Blocks - One Layer Cake (24 - 10" squares)

From 12 - 10" squares cut: 3 - 2 ⅞" squares (36 total)	F
2 - 2 ⅞" squares (24 total)	G
From 12 - 10" squares: 1 - 10" square (12 total)	H

Outer Borders - ½ yard

1 - 2 ½" x WOF strip, subcut into: 2 - 2 ½" x 18 ½" strips	I
3 - 2 ½" x WOF strips, sew end to end and subcut into: 2 - 2 ½" x 56 ½" strips	J

Binding - ½ yard

5 - 2 ½" x WOF strips	K

Pieced Backing - ½ yard

2 - 6" x WOF strips, sew end to end and subcut into: 1 - 6" x 57 ½" strip	L

Sparkling Star Blocks:

Draw a diagonal line on the wrong side of the Fabric C squares.

With right sides facing, layer a Fabric C square with a Fabric G square.

Stitch ¼" from each side of the drawn line.

Cut apart on the marked line.

Half Square Triangle Unit should measure 2 ½" x 2 ½".

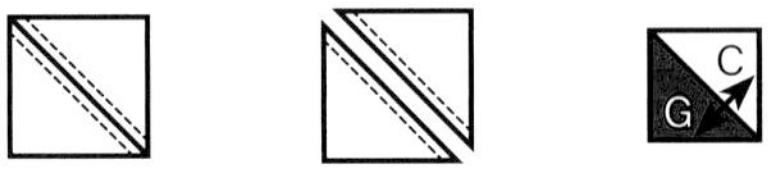

Make forty-eight.

Cut the Fabric A squares and Fabric F squares on the diagonal once.

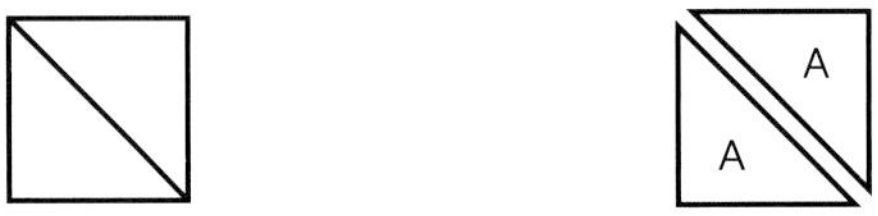

Make thirty-six.

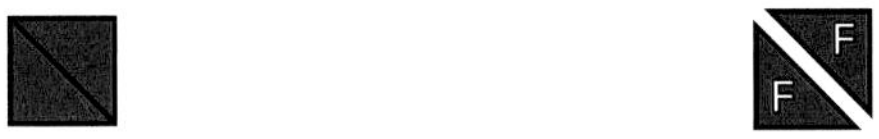

Make seventy-two.

Assemble Unit using matching fabric. Press open.
Sparkling Star Unit should measure 4 ½" x 4 ½".

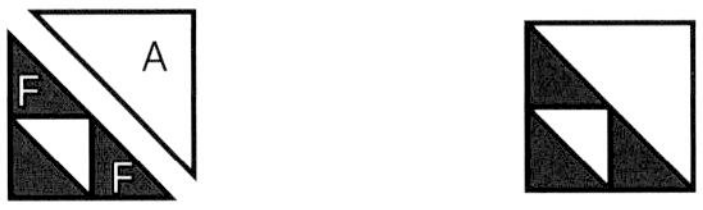

Make thirty-six.
You will not use all Half Square Triangle Units.

semble Block. Press open.

arkling Star Block should measure 16 ½" x 16 ½".

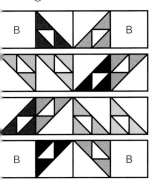

ke three.

able Runner Assembly:

semble Tablerunner Center using Fabric D strips for sashing. Press toward the background.

ble Runner Center should measure 16 ½" x 50 ½".

ach side inner borders using the remaining Fabric D strips.

ach top and bottom inner borders using the Fabric E strips.

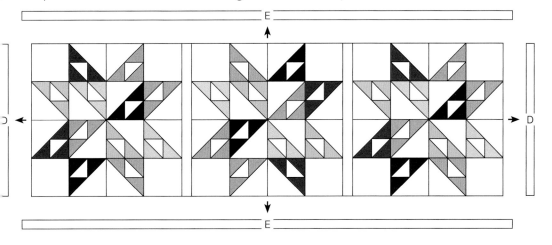

Wish Table Runner

Attach side outer borders using the Fabric I strips.

Attach top and bottom outer borders using the Fabric J strips.

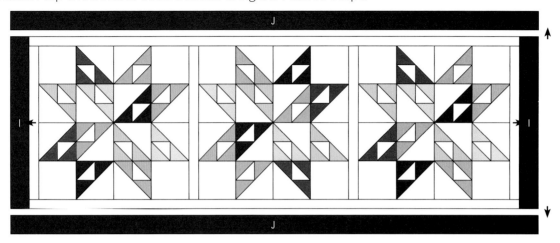

Pieced Backing:

Assemble Pieced Backing.

Pieced Backing should measure 25" x 57 ½".

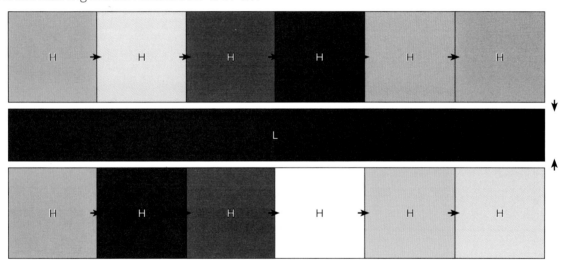

Finishing:

Piece the Fabric K strips end to end for binding.

Quilt and bind as desired.

A Few of Bonnie & Camille's Favorite Things:

We are simple girls that don't use a lot of notions and quilting supplies and usually stick to our tried and true favorites. Here are a few of them. Maybe there's one you'd like to try?

Camille

· My Juki TL-2000Qi
· Aurifil 50wt thread in color 2024
· Warm & White cotton batting
· 6 ½" Bloc-Loc Half Square Triangle Ruler
· We used Moda's Bella Solid Off White (SKU# 9900-200) in most of the quilts in this book!

Bonnie

· My 20 year old Bernina 1080
· Reliable Velocity 200IR Iron
· Leather thimble pads for hand binding
· Magnetic pin bowls

Camille's Beehive Quilt

Pieced by Camille Roskelley, Bonnie Olaveson and all the quilters on pages 54 to 57
Quilted by Abby Latimer
Fabric from various Bonnie & Camille collections for Moda Fabrics

Beehive Quilts

I started sharing my quilting projects on my family blog back in 2006. I didn't have any local quilting friends at the time and thought I just might be the only 23-year-old quilter out there. I will never forget the first comment I received on one of my quilt posts from a fellow quilter all the way across the country. It was so exciting to connect with someone in the same stage of life that was also making quilts. Things just continued to grow from there as more and more quilting blogs started popping up, Flickr groups and quilt alongs formed, and then our amazing Instagram community started to take shape. Now there are hundreds of thousands of quilters online sharing their beautiful projects and encouraging other quilters. The generosity and love shown by these quilting friends is truly an inspiration. So much good has been done by so many of you!

In January I asked our Instagram friends if they would help us with a project for this book by making a little 3 ½" block or two. We wondered if we would get 100, but crossed our fingers hoping to get enough to make a 72" quilt. Checking the post office box became my favorite part of the day, and I would spend hours reading cards and letters, recording names and sorting all the beautiful blocks by color. More than once I was brought to tears while reading your kind words.

A few short weeks later we had enough blocks for two large quilts made from 1,076 blocks made by 583 quilters from 11 countries, 48 states and by two supportive husbands. It was an amazing community effort, and these quilts will forever be our very favorites. A beehive is a symbol of industry, a reminder that together, when we all contribute something small, it turns into something so much bigger than any of us. And that is exactly what this project, what our online quilting community, is. We are so lucky to be a small part of it.

Camille

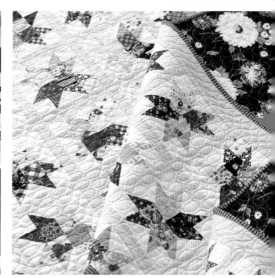

Camille's Beehive Quilt

LAP Cutting Instructions:

Background - 1 ⅞ yards

15 - 2 ½" x WOF strips, subcut into:	
228 - 2 ½" squares	A
12 - 2" x WOF strips, subcut into:	
228 - 2" squares	B

Blocks - One Layer Cake (38 - 10" squares)

From each 10" square:	
6 - 2 ½" squares (228 total)	C
6 - 2" squares (228 total)	D

Sashing & Borders - 1 ⅓ yards

8 - 1 ½" x WOF strips, subcut into:	
48 - 1 ½" x 6 ½" rectangles	E
9 - 1 ½" x WOF strips, sew end to end and subcut into:	
7 - 1 ½" x 48 ½" strips	F
6 - 2 ½" x WOF strips, sew end to end and subcut into:	
2 - 2 ½" x 55 ½" strips	G
2 - 2 ½" x 52 ½" strips	H

Binding - ⅝ yard

7 - 2 ½" x WOF strips	I

Backing - 3 ½ yards

TWIN Cutting Instructions:

Background - 3 ⅓ yards

27 - 2 ½" x WOF strips, subcut into:	
432 - 2 ½" squares	A
22 - 2" x WOF strips, subcut into:	
432 - 2" squares	B

Blocks - Two Layer Cakes (72 - 10" squares)

From each 10" square:	
6 - 2 ½" squares (432 total)	C
6 - 2" squares (432 total)	D

Sashing & Borders - 2 ¼ yards

16 - 1 ½" x WOF strips, subcut into:	
96 - 1 ½" x 6 ½" rectangles	E
18 - 1 ½" x WOF strips, sew end to end and subcut into:	
11 - 1 ½" x 62 ½" strips	F
9 - 2 ½" x WOF strips, sew end to end and subcut into:	
2 - 2 ½" x 83 ½" strips	G
2 - 2 ½" x 66 ½" strips	H

Binding - ⅞ yard

9 - 2 ½" x WOF strips	I

Backing - 5 ½ yards

Block Swaps:

In August of 2015, after seeing Lissa Alexander host a log cabin swap amongst friends, I decided to launch a Bonnie and Camille version of a block swap on Instagram. I adored the idea of sharing this hobby with so many friends and having a piece of them in a quilt to cherish forever. I had no idea how many people would also be excited about the project as I was. The response to this swap was incredible. The premise was to make 12 - 24" log cabin blocks with Bonnie and Camille fabrics. Then cut the blocks into quarters, save one quarter of each block for themselves and mail the remaining quarters to me. I would then package up 36 different blocks to mail back to each participant. We received over 3,700 blocks by the time the swap concluded. Quilters from 42 states in the USA and 10 countries around the world participated in the most amazing swap ever. The #bclogcabinswapfun on Instagram is filled with over 900 posts of quilters taking their blocks and creating beautiful quilts of all different configurations from blocks exchanged with 36 fellow quilters who love Bonnie and Camille fabrics. Being a quilter is such a special hobby on its own, but sharing a common bond of hobby and fabric to create quilts together as friends across thousands of miles is something I'll never forget.

Samantha Olsen
(Instagram: @samanthaleeolsen)

QUEEN Cutting Instructions:

Background - 5 ⅛ yards

43 - 2 ½" x WOF strips, subcut into:	
678 - 2 ½" squares	A
34 - 2" x WOF strips, subcut into:	
676 - 2" squares	B

Blocks - Three Layer Cakes (113 - 10" squares)

From each 10" square:	
6 - 2 ½" squares (678 total)	C
6 - 2" squares (678 total)	D

Sashing & Borders - 3 ⅛ yards

26 - 1 ½" x WOF strips, subcut into:	
156 - 1 ½" x 6 ½" rectangles	E
29 - 1 ½" x WOF strips, sew end to end and subcut into:	
12 - 1 ½" x 90 ½" strips	F
10 - 2 ½" x WOF strips, sew end to end and subcut into:	
2 - 2 ½" x 90 ½" strips	G
2 - 2 ½" x 94 ½" strips	H

Binding - 1 yard

11 - 2 ½" x WOF strips	I

Backing - 8 ¾ yards

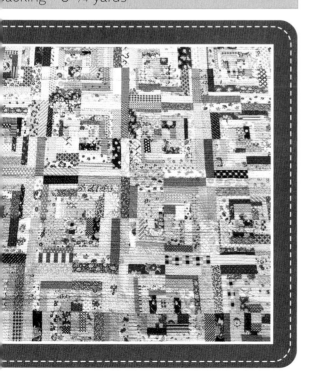

Beehive Blocks:

Each Corner Unit uses two color coordinating 10" squares.

Draw a diagonal line on the wrong side of the Fabric A squares.

With right sides facing, layer a Fabric A square with a Fabric C square.

Stitch ¼" from each side of the drawn line.

Cut apart on the marked line.

TRIM Half Square Triangle Unit to measure 2" x 2".

LAP: Make 456.
TWIN: Make 864.
QUEEN: Make 1,356.

Assemble Unit using color coordinating fabric. Press open.

Corner Unit should measure 3 ½" x 3 ½".

LAP: Make 228.
TWIN: Make 432.
QUEEN: Make 676. You will not use all Half Square Triangle Units and Fabric D squares.

Assemble Block. Press open.

Beehive Block should measure 6 ½" x 6 ½".

LAP: Make 57.
TWIN: Make 108.
QUEEN: Make 169.

Camille's Beehive Quilt

LAP Quilt Assembly:

Assemble Lap Quilt Center using Fabric E rectangles and Fabric F strips as sashing. You will not use one Beehive Block. Press toward the sashing.

Lap Quilt Center should measure 48 ½" x 55 ½".

Attach side borders using the Fabric G strips.

Attach top and bottom borders using the Fabric H strips.

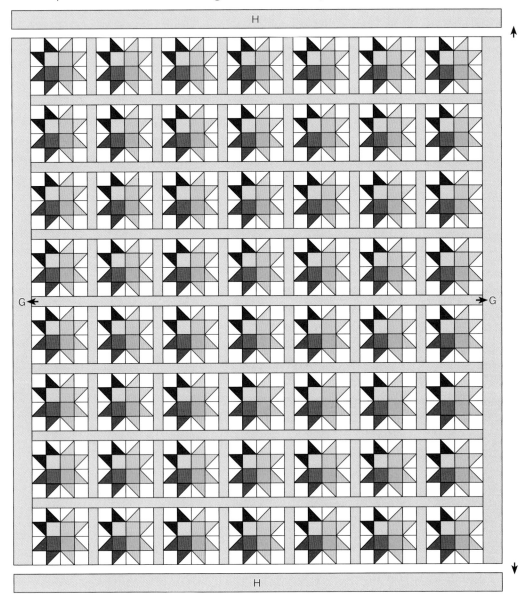

LAP Finishing:

Piece the Fabric I strips end to end for binding.

Quilt and bind as desired.

TWIN Quilt Assembly:

Assemble Twin Quilt Center using Fabric E rectangles and Fabric F strips as sashing. Press toward the sashing.
Twin Quilt Center should measure 62 ½" x 83 ½".
Attach side borders using the Fabric G strips.
Attach top and bottom borders using the Fabric H strips.

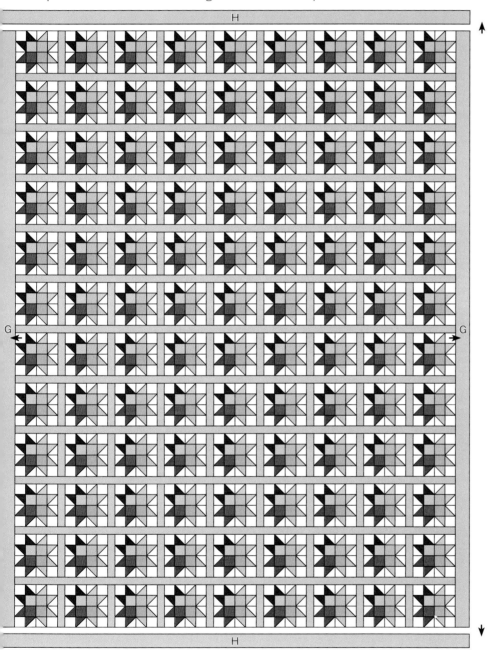

TWIN Finishing:

Piece the Fabric I strips end to end for binding.
Quilt and bind as desired.

Camille's Beehive Quilt

QUEEN Quilt Assembly:

Assemble Queen Quilt Center using Fabric E rectangles and Fabric F strips as sashing. Press toward the sashing.

Queen Quilt Center should measure 90 ½" x 90 ½".

Attach side borders using the Fabric G strips.

Attach top and bottom borders using the Fabric H strips.

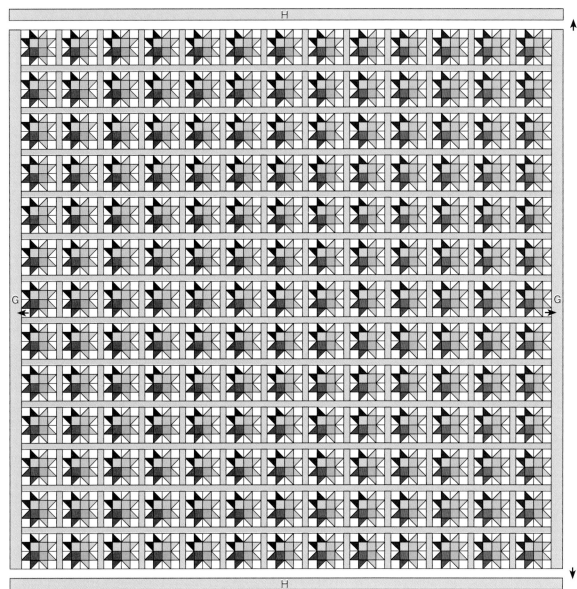

QUEEN Finishing:

Piece the Fabric I strips end to end for binding.

Quilt and bind as desired.

Bonnie's Beehive Quilt

Pieced by Bonnie Olaveson, Camille Roskelley and all the quilters on pages 54 to 57
Quilted by Susan Hansen
Fabric from various Bonnie & Camille collections for Moda Fabrics

Finding Your Quilting Tribe Online:

Making quilting friends is just a click away thanks to the supportive and awesome quilting community on Instagram. When I started quilting, I turned to Instagram for inspiration and was pleasantly surprised to find so many like-minded people sharing their quilts, favorite techniques and words of encouragement.

If you want to find your tribe online:

- **Start with your Favorites** Search the hashtags of your favorite quilting techniques, types of quilts, fabric designers, quilt patterns and any other quilting related favorites so that you can interact and form a bond with quilters who like the same things you do.

- **Leave Comments** Forming a friendship requires interaction, so before you hit that like button and move on, take a moment to leave a comment about what you like on the post. As you share and interact, friendships begin to form.

- **Post your Photos** People can't befriend you if they don't know you, so be sure to share photos of your quilts along with relevant hashtags. Hashtags allow other quilters to discover you when they are searching for their favorites. Without hashtags it is much harder for people to find you to form connections.

- **Participate in Swaps and Quilt Alongs** Participating in the various swaps and quilt alongs hosted on Instagram is a great way to interact with other quilters who like the same things you do. Funny enough, I have met in "real life" and befriended more than half of the people I have swapped mini quilts with.

Almost all of my quilting friendships started on Instagram, so go log in and find your tribe.

Megan Dunton, Monograms for Makers
(Instagram: @monogramsformakers / @thebaconandmegsews)

Bonnie's Beehive Quilt

Cutting Instructions:

Background & Inner Borders - 4 ½ yards

25 - 2 ½" x WOF strips, subcut into:
    400 - 2 ½" squares   A

27 - 2" x WOF strips, subcut into:
    20 - 2" x 12 ½" rectangles   B
    400 - 2" squares   C

8 - 2 ½" x WOF strips, sew end to end and subcut into:
    2 - 2 ½" x 66 ½" strips   D
    2 - 2 ½" x 70 ½" strips   E

8 - 2" x WOF strips, sew end to end and subcut into:
    4 - 2" x 66 ½" strips   F

Blocks - Two Layer Cakes (50 - 10" squares)

From each 10" square:
    8 - 2 ½" squares (400 total)   G
    8 - 2" squares (400 total)   H

Outer Borders - 1 ½ yards

9 - 5" x WOF strips, sew end to end and subcut into:
    2 - 5" x 70 ½" strips   I
    2 - 5" x 79 ½" strips   J

Binding - ⅞ yard

    9 - 2 ½" x WOF strips   K

Backing - 7 ½ yards

Beehive Blocks:

Each Beehive Block uses color coordinating 10" squares.

Draw a diagonal line on the wrong side of the Fabric A squares.

With right sides facing, layer a Fabric A square with a Fabric G square.

Stitch ¼" from each side of the drawn line.

Cut apart on the marked line.

TRIM Half Square Triangle Unit to measure 2" x 2".

Make eight hundred.

Assemble Unit using color coordinating fabric. Press open.

Corner Unit should measure 3 ½" x 3 ½".

Make four hundred.

...ssemble Unit using color coordinating fabric. Press
...pen.

...eehive Unit should measure 6 ½" x 6 ½".

...ake one hundred.

...ssemble Block using color coordinating fabric. Press
...pen.

...eehive Block should measure 12 ½" x 12 ½".

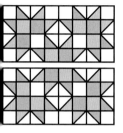 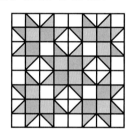

...ake twenty-five.

Bonnie's Beehive Quilt

Quilt Assembly:

Assemble Quilt Center using Fabric B rectangles and Fabric F strips for sashing. Press toward the sashing.

Quilt Center should measure 66 ½" x 66 ½".

Attach side inner borders using the Fabric D strips.

Attach top and bottom inner borders using the Fabric E strips.

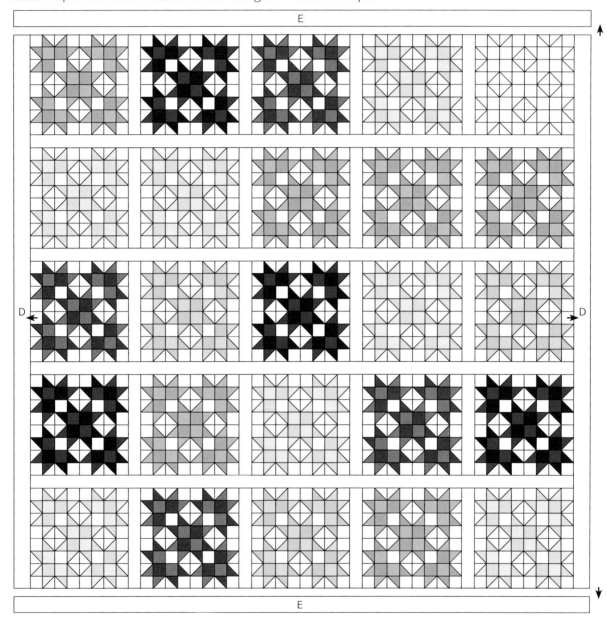

tach side outer borders using the Fabric I strips.
tach top and bottom outer borders using the Fabric J strips.

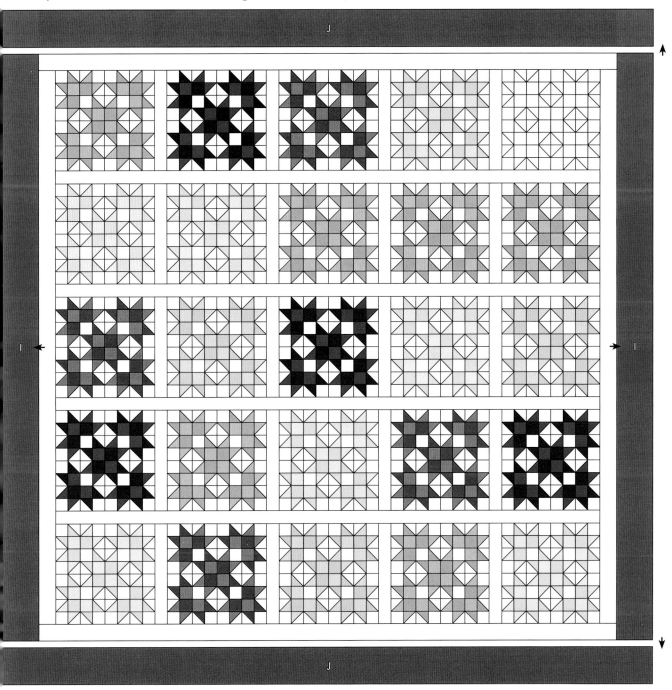

inishing:

ce the Fabric K strips end to end for binding.
ilt and bind as desired.

Beehive Quilt Contributors:

Janice Rampton, UT
Heidi Carpenter, NE
Tina Skinner, UT
Elaine Rottman, CA
Suzanne Kolhagen, CT
Julia Scriven, CA
Hailey Berkstresser, PA
Judy Morgan, MI
Teresa Gottwig, NC
Rachel Ricks, NV
Dawn Derrick, TX
Martha Thompson, KY
Jana Kigin, PA
Charity Giasson, RI
Debbie Aldridge, ID
Mary Stiver, MS
Lauren Markham, MD
Stephanie Ashton, UT
Diane VanRyn, SC
Melissa Foster, OK
Nancy Rognholt, MN
Andrea Thomson, UT
Rachel Eaton, MI
Ginger Peterson, AZ
Heather Briggs, KS
Laura Moore, GA
Debbie Taylor, TX
Hollie Kimber, UT
Amy Lawrence, CA
Mary Ives, MA
Rachel Eaton, MI
Leisha Farnsworth, UT
Donna Sturm, TX
Kirsten McPeck, OH
Carolyn Skinner, UT
Kathleen Leger, CA
Dawn Davs, WA
Sherry Meabon, PA
Beth Neperud, CO
Stephanie Johnson, CA
Judy Zoll, MO
Julie Thompson, NY

Mary Andra Holmes
Jo Ellen Stevens, OH
Pat Heney, OH
Janie Farmer, KY
Donna Cole-Beyer, AZ
Angie Cruse, WA
Ally Dupre', LA
Danna Murnyack, ND
Megan Salter, GA
Debbie Frio, MA
Whitney Leonard
Christina Johnson, NH
Jenny Schwab, IL
Josie King, ID
Angie King, WA
Edie Frasier, FL
Dawn Defeo, CT
Gaye Larsen, CA
Margie Hirst, UT
Amy Edgemon, TN
Amanda Little, NC
Samantha Gillam, MS
Jessica Vetor, KY
Sara Cecil, TN
Cheryl Overland, MN
Kris Busch, AR
Lacey Winn, OK
Suzanne Hampton, TX
Ilka Moosman, Brazil
Annalee Kennedy, UT
Jolee Sisney, MO
Lacey Winn, OK
Camille LeFebvre, NY
Jona Poore
Lisa Donnelly, MO
Janine Scott
Erin Kern, IA
Linda Adkins, AR
Laura Brown, SC
Betsy Updegrave, PA
Ariel Davis, IN
Jessica F. , IN

Kelly Meanix, PA
Marlia Gordon, ID
Amy Cunnington, ID
Sue Miller, CA
Tonya Sherman, CA
Kari Reed, CA
Samantha Ngo, CA
Yolanda Carmona, WI
Chris O'Dorisio, VA
Treesa Porter, ID
LeAnne Ballard, AZ
Diana Wylie, TX
Misty West, TX
Wanda Richardson, IA
Reitha Hall, OR
Mary Kolb, MN
Alissa Strouse, CA
Christy Johnson, WA
Laura Bair, PA
Amber Lowell, VA
JaNean Frandsen, UT
Rebecca Sherwood, TX
Laurel Horchem, UT
Bea Dockter, FL
Gwen Sager, CT
Emilee Hathaway, UT
Martha Penner Novacek, OK
Peggy Raines, OR
Jaylene Britt, UT
Miranda Dilschneider, Canada
Lesa Brown, TX
Tammy White, WV
Peggy Raines, OR
Shannon Stewart, WA
Peggy Aront, NJ
Ashley Whitcomb, MN
Katy Greenfield, OK
Jodi Smith, FL
Diane Keach
Toni Maxwell
Elizabeth Lakey, AL

Brooke Lakey, AL
Danette Miller, ID
Julie Mortenson, NV
Beth Shreve, IN
Jan Bracha, OR
Mary Jo Poole, MS
Mary Bailey, CA
Ann Weber, VA
Sherry E. Riggs, KY
Kristen Loudenburg, CO
Julie Gehman, AL
Michelle High, AK
Linda Wade, FL
Shelly Peterson, AK
Margo Sosinski, NV
Kristin Leandro, HI
Patricia Newhouse, TX
Chris Mott, TX
Laurel Fletchtner, VA
Amber Laulainen, AK
Christine Weld, NY
Paige English, AZ
Sandy Carter, WA
Elaine Satterfield
Kimberly Nagle, KS
Jennilyn Landry, CO
Yvonne Ketterman, CA
Paulette Bowman, IL
April Lopez, TX
Natalie Grange, UT
Amy Griffiths, UT
Elena Cultra
Trish Collins
Pat Conely, MN
Amanda Wilbert, TX
Annie Green, GA
Kim Arrowood, GA
Mansa Larsen, UT
Deanne Dye Bolinder
Tammy Menlove, UT
Naudia Tatum, OH
Candy Lamers, MO

hris Floraday, MI
ebi Chipps, WV
ancy Denny, NC
ris Vine, CA
aren Sousa, RI
ue Winter, UT
arbara Hand, OH
herilyn Dunn, OH
sa Burns, OH
icole Scott, CO
orrie Munson, ID
m McArthur, AZ
arcy Oren, WA
ancy Chavez, OR
iriam Moore, TX
heryl Hannah, MO
artha Farner, PA
ora Keck, IN
mona O'Loughlin, MN
retchen Sanders, TX
ean Cameron, NC
l Hammon, WA
indy Hawkins, Australia
nna Friedt, ND
aren Davis, Australia
ennifer Bergeron, LA
ichele Raiola, NY
onya Mullis, VA
rica Walrath, MT
anell Cline, CA
ichele Sutton, AR
ari Lynn Smith, SD
haron Henson, CA
andy Bruns, NC
helly Davey-West, CA
ndsey Henderson, MT
ebecca Orlowski, PA
ary Ann Scanlon
nna Graber, KS
cki Longing, AR
nn Marie Veara, MD
borrah Allen, AZ

Janice Duprey, NY
Allison Glover, MS
Shannon Cogswell, CA
Paula Ellingson, TX
Carolyn Sands, TX
Judeyanne Coudrain, LA
Kate Balogh, IL
Tsvetana Schmolke, UT
Andrea Johnson, IN
Bryce Hiener, OH
Joyce Joy, OH
Heather Lyon, CT
Amy Brondyke, OH
Paula Fairchild, MO
Kaci Peterson, MO
Denise Ruddell, ID
Hildy Ebertzeder, Germany
Debbie Miner, MS
Theresa Maddox, TN
Norma Goggin, Ireland
Janice Spring, CA
Susan Jahncke, IL
Patti Garner, IL
Kim Courtright, PA
Theresa Terry, UT
Beth Wright, MI
Melissa Corry, UT
Jessica Harris, WA
Anna Marie Short, MO
Teresa Evenhouse, IL
Elly Evenhouse, MI
Christine Carlson, NV
Sonia Herdman, ID
Cecilia Corry, UT
Julie Washburn, FL
Debby Maples, TN
Donna Fanning, MS
Diane LeCompte, DE
Anne Savarese, NC
Catherine DiNardo, PA
Kim Hensley, OH
K. Rainwater, OR

Amanda Smith, MN
Carol Lewis, AZ
Marcia Baker, SC
Lindsey Stelly, LA
Charlene Schuster, AZ
Deidra McCollum, WA
Jude Jones, ID
Anita Bigley, VA
Tania Craddock, GA
Sherry Varley, UT
Nancy Fitzpatrick, TX
Kathy Tuttle, CA
Carrie Bogle, TX
Kimberly Walus, UT
Sarah Whitmey, Japan
Stephanie Billeaud, LA
Paula Hampton, OR
Jennifer Kalt, TX
Misti Creach, OK
Kathy Roma, NY
Rita Mulvey, CT
Sharon Smith, PA
Tonia Zeiler, MO
Jessie Lathroum, TX
Paige Johnson, AZ
Hanna Chupp, GA
Chris Lewellen
Bethany DeWitt, ID
Karen Storey, Canada
Helen Grieve, WA
Patty Allee, IL
Jenifer Lake, SC
Anna Skelton, WA
Kylie Buttigieg, Australia
Alisa Arveseth, UT
Corinna Burrows, Australia
Lynn Nowak, OH
Gloria Pingry, GA
Ellen Fischer, CA
Debi Henry, VT
Karrissa Johnson, VA
Mindy Hulst, MI

Marge Mulder, MI
Nancy DeMaagd, MI
Katherine Rose, UT
Romney Ludgate, WI
Nancy Costa, NJ
Shannah Mallich, TN
Terri Boyd, Canada
Brooke Riggs, KY
Bonnie Fredmund, UT
Kristy Lucey, MI
Terrie Galle, KS
Ange Davied, KS
Gail Staehle, FL
Rebecca Rico, WA
Karly Leidig, MI
Debbie Jeske, WA
Anne Gerhart, NC
Simone Kraling, The Netherlands
Christina Sutter, TX
Marjorie Ford, Canada
Sandra Schnodhorst, Germany
Cindy Johansen, CA
Betsy Smith, PA
Anna Lester, AR
Brenda Beyer, WA
Dee Knudsen, CA
Kim McIntyre, Australia
Clara Chandler, WA
Beth Wright, MI
Rachel Provencher, NH
Rachel Moffett, GA
Natalie Morgan, MA
LeAnne Kehoe, CA
Becky Hoss, CA
Cami Groethe, UT
Debbie Vannette, MI
Kathleen Mason, NC
Julia Schembari, NY
Jan Sessions, TX
Jane Graham, NV
Dianna Martinez, TX

Beehive Quilt Contributors:

Stephanie Hoffman, Canada
Shirley Willis, Australia
Lynn Morris, NJ
Debbie Hamilton, AZ
Jennifer Heaton, TN
Tammy Pollock, OH
Laura Walkup, NV
Janee Bell, AZ
Donna Allen, AZ
Margaret Sudweeks, CA
Bethanie DeGayner, MI
Judith Wiggins, Australia
Deb Tyson, Australia
Chris Panos, CA
Dana Schmitt, PA
Kristin Renfro, PA
Nancy Burrill, MA
Vicki Tucek, Australia
Zoe Green, Australia
Elaine Richins, UT
Brenda Hotinger, GA
Susan Ottem, GA

Sheryl Kouche, AZ
Lynn Maple, NV
Sally Matoushek, TX
Becky Keizer, Canada
Joan Anderson, Canada
Olivia Worthington, NJ
Nicole Worthington, NJ
Kim Michniak, PA
Cat Demack, Australia
Karen Hall, TN
Carla Flood, IL
Robin Veltema, MI
Dawn Veltema, MI
Rebecca Padding, MI
Faye Gareau, Canada
Bobbie Badovick, OH
Suzy Dimouski, Australia
Irene Llere, TX
Frances Anderson, NM
Melanie McCarthy, Canada
Janine Bennett, Australia
Diana Dyer, GA
Deb Girotti, VA

Claire Fisher, Australia
Pat Ravenberg, UT
Aniva Willouhby, UT
Cheryl Koethe, VA
Rina Huettner, NV
Stephanie Pattison, NV
Catalina Solano, Canada
Mathilde Nelson, CO
Roslyn McGovern, Australia
Nikki Kelly, Australia
Karen Notley, Australia
Cindy Deatsman, WA
Melissa Dryer, UT
Karen Sanford, UT
Andrea Peters, AK
Gayle Bamnerlin, KY
Barb Boggs, OH
Kim Adams, UT
Abby Adams, UT
Marcia Archer, VA
Makenzie Erker, KS
Lindsay Castleman, OK
Sally Nielson, ID

Karen Rodriguez, TX
Kamee Groethe, UT
Judy Ballou, UT
Sharon Stone, TX
Pris Phillips, ID
Lorraine Houghton, WA
Janee Walkup Bell, AZ
Kristen McCollor, MN
Sheila Clark, SD
Elizabeth Vogt, SD
Clarice Blumer, SD
Renee Wald, SD
Sara Green, SD
Jenny Williams, SD
Kate Spellman, SD
Lily Mitchell, SD
Ila Johnson, UT
Carol Beesley, ID
Laura Swenson, NY
Karen Johns, IL
Cindy Hilfiger, PA
Christy Taylor, ID
Caitlin Preston, Canada

osemary Farmer, MA
anean Landa, ND
m Cleland, AR
ylissa Gholson, TX
acey Poirier, MT
eresa Shover, WA
obyn Christie, IN
va Mancini, FL
lison Mancini, FL
usie Greer, KS
etsy Kise, AZ
eeAnn McDowell, TX
herry Travis, OH
lly Kiel, CO
nnifer Arguijo, TX
shley Spitler
harlene Cagle
erena Mullins, Australia
m West, TX
atharine Hehrer, MI
usan Oler, UT
atie Kwiatkowski, MI
ngie Finn, Australia
harla Krenzel, KS
ndi Luethge, NE
Belk, AR
eth Burden, AR
shley Altizer, OH
usy Jones, UT
esley Boland, Australia
ichele Amstutz, FL
aren Diedrich, WI
usan Vaughan, CA
ebecca Woods, Australia
ta Jane Cowan, Australia
ichele Hellman, KY
ren Pearson, VA
tie Winkelman, WI
hris Clingingsmith, IL
annah Wetterstrom, TX
nda Stemmermann, TX
thie Dye, NV

Michelle Arnold Nitengale, OR
Adriana VanRyn, FL
Hayley Fershtut, UT
Pat Blowers, AZ
Julia Davis, CO
Ellie Davis, CO
Sarah Rothe, Australia
Christine Van Berkel, Australia
Jenny Pilkington, UK
Anne-Lize Berg, The Netherlands
Paula Francis, Canada
Cynthia Reaves, MS
Christine Jenks, WA
Chrys Smethwick, MI
Samantha Smethwick, MI
Arlene Lehman, MI
Donna Rutten, MO
Melinda France, Australia
Marie Johansson, Tokyo
Stephanie Mitchell, AZ
Lisa Gonzalez, NY
Jennifer Creech, VA
Sachiko Phillips, Australia
Carla Vancamp, Canada
Lorraine Vermeer, Canada
Gina Growe, IL
Lynn Hinson, FL
Brigid York, UT
Shannon Leathers, OK
Sheila Boser, AR
Phyllis Beesley Moss, ID
Alana Lerwill, ID
Aloma Bowen, ID
Mark Olaveson, ID
Jarom Roskelley, NV
Jennifer Bumps, IN
Karyn Sullivan, Canada
Doris Maxwell, Canada
Mardeen Libby, CO
Nancy Thornberg, MN

Sherry Johnson, GA
Diane Hawn, MT
Paula Hall, TX
Donna Bradshaw, KY
Catherine Gill, Canada
Marcie Koch, WA
Connie Koch, WA
Shandiin Schwendiman, WA
Cara Morrill, WA
Zoee Deruwe, WA
Cheyenne Schwendiman, WA
Diane Flakelar, Australia
Rosemary Fox, Australia
Kim Barnett, WA
Kori Ritola, CA
Katherine, AR
Kim Brydson-Dixon, Australia
LeeAnn McMahon, AL
Kristin Moore, IL
Karen Seafert
Liz Henselmeier, CA
Christie Norman, MI
Brenda Norris, FL
Suzann Huff, TN
Michelle Spell, SC
Abby Hinrichs, MN
Becky Hinrichs, MN
Stacey Hinrichs, MN
Michelle Carter, Canada
Charlotte M Castine, IL
Gina Campbell, RI
CarolAnn Hawkins, CA
Martha Narino-Torres, AK
Kitty Materanek, TX
Mary Lorber, MO
Linda Rising, AZ
Brenda Way, OR
Maren Kuhnert, Germany
Antje Schmiedecke, Germany

Nicole Roche Zeisler
Jayne Bromley
Pat Crossman, Canada
Jen Norman, Jersey
Kim Monins, Jersey
Sue Bone, Jersey
Sarah Matlock, Jersey
Jacqueline Tardivel, Jersey
Jill Day, Jersey
Jenny Marshall, Jersey
Sue Harris, Jersey
Val L., Jersey
Kathy J., Jersey
Amanda Colledge
Vivienne Rees
Gill Hancox
Gay Casper, MN
Katrin N., Germany
Fabienne N., Germany
Nicole Christoffersen, UT
Marilyn Mayfield, OK
Kassi Gibson, OK
Katrina Williams, OK
Pat Bedont, UT
Jaci Bedont, UT
Kathy Duerksen, Canada
Carmela Zenga, Italy
Sara Casebolt, FL
Collin Casebolt, FL
Shirley Johnson Hagan, KY
Stefanie Williams, TN
Natalie Colbourne, Canada
Diana Brown, England
Kimalee Portalupi, UT

A very heartfelt thank you to all of you again. We love you all!

- Bonnie & Camille

Beehive Pillow

Made by Bonnie Olaveson

Fabric from various Bonnie & Camille collections for Moda Fabrics

Beehive Pillow

A few days after we put out the request for Beehive quilt blocks (and long before we knew we'd have enough for two quilts!), the cutest little blocks started arriving at Camille's house. She was having so much fun with them that I decided I needed to whip up a few of my own to play with. One afternoon I made 16 units and sewed them together into a single colorful star. I decided it would make a perfect pillow for the window seat in my sewing room, and I couldn't stop until I was done. Making pillows out of favorite quilt blocks has always been something I enjoyed, and this one was particularly delightful to stitch. Sometimes you just don't have the extra time needed to make a whole quilt, but sewing a quick pillow can brighten your home and your day while still letting you feel creative. Start with this pillow and then make a pillow for each of the Shine On Sampler quilt blocks. You'll have a house full of happy pillows in no time!

— *Bonnie*

Beehive Pillow

Cutting Instructions:

Scrappy Backgrounds - Fat Quarter or Scraps	
2 - 2 ½" x 21" strips, subcut into: 16 - 2 ½" squares	A
2 - 2" x 21" strips, subcut into: 16 - 2" squares	B
Blocks - One Mini Charm Pack **(32 - 2 ½" squares)**	
From 16 - 2 ½" squares: 1 - 2 ½" square (16 total)	C
From 16 - 2 ½" squares cut: 1 - 2" square (16 total)	D
Borders - ⅜ yard	

2 - 4 ½" x WOF strips, subcut into:
    2 - 4 ½" x 12 ½" strips
    2 - 4 ½" x 20 ½" strips
	E
	F

Pillow Back - ⅔ yard	

1 - 19" x WOF strip, subcut into:
    1 - 17 ½" x 19" rectangle
    1 - 4" x 19" rectangle
	G
	H

Muslin - ⅔ yard	
1 - 21 ½" square	
Batting - craft size	
1 - 21 ½" square	
Zipper	
1 - 20" zipper	
18" Pillow Form	

Another Idea:
Navy and White

Quilted Pillow Front:

Each Corner Unit uses color coordinating prints.

Draw a diagonal line on the wrong side of the Fabric A squares.

With right sides facing, layer a Fabric A square with a Fabric C square.

Stitch ¼" from each side of the drawn line.

Cut apart on the marked line.

TRIM Half Square Triangle Unit to measure 2" x 2".

Make thirty-two.

Assemble Unit using color coordinating fabric. Press open.

Corner Unit should measure 3 ½" x 3 ½".

Make sixteen.

Assemble Unit. Press open.

Beehive Unit should measure 6 ½" x 6 ½".

Make four.

Assemble Block. Press open.

Beehive Block should measure 12 ½" x 12 ½".

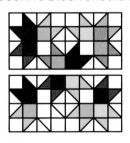 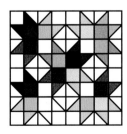

Make one.

...tach side borders using the Fabric E strips.

...tach top and bottom borders using the Fabric F
...rips.

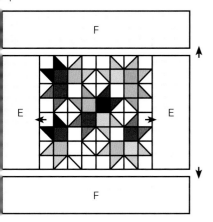

...ake one.

...yer the Pillow Front, the Batting and the Muslin
...uare.

...uilt as desired.

...RIM Pillow Front to measure 19" x 19".

...aste 1/8" around the inside of the Quilted Pillow Front.

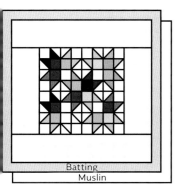

...ake one.

illow Back:

...th wrong sides together, fold the Fabric H rectangle
...half.

...ing a topstitch, attach the zipper to the folded
...bric H rectangle.

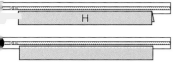

...ake one Bottom Pillow Back.

With right sides facing, attach the Bottom Pillow Back
to the Fabric G rectangle.

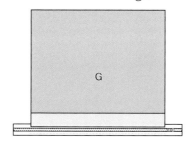

To create the zipper cover, fold and press the Fabric G
rectangle 1/2" away from the bottom edge.

Topstitch the folded zipper cover in place.

Move the zipper pull to the center of the Pillow Back.

TRIM Pillow Back to measure 19" x 19".

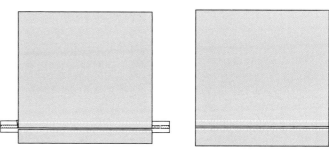

Make one.

Pillow Finishing:

With right sides facing, layer the Quilted Pillow Front
with the Pillow Back. Pin in place.

Sew 1/2" around the edges.

Turn right side out and insert the pillow form.

Zip pillow closed.

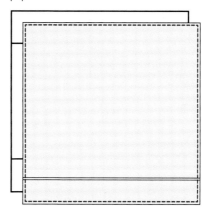

Good Times Quilt

Pieced by Camille Roskelley
Quilted by Abby Latimer
Fabric from At Home by Bonnie & Camille for Moda Fabrics

Good Times Quilt

More often than not, I sew alone in my sewing room with my two cats, Cosmo and Stitch, to keep me company. I love my sewing space; I love that I can listen to my favorite music, a great podcast or just enjoy a few moments of peace and quiet after a busy day. I make quilts because I love the entire process, and as an introvert, this kind of creativity just feels so essential. I sew a lot of quilt samples for new fabric collections and new patterns, but when I'm not doing that, I'm usually sewing something for someone I love. A new baby, a birthday, a special thank you, a Christmas gift, there are just so many occasions that need a special quilt in that special person's favorite colors. I love that even though I may be sewing alone, the quilts I make and send out into the world keep my loved ones warm and make them feel loved wherever they are.

— Camille

Good Times Quilt

TABLE TOPPER
Cutting Instructions:

Background & Borders - 1 yard	
4 - 5" x WOF strips, subcut into: 32 - 5" squares	A

4 - 2 ½" x WOF strips, subcut into:
   2 - 2 ½" x 32 ½" strips
   2 - 2 ½" x 36 ½" strips
	B
	C

Blocks - One Charm Pack (32 - 5" squares)	
From 24 - 5" squares: 1 - 5" square (24 total)	D
From 8 - 5" squares: 1 - 5" square (8 total)	E
Binding - ½ yard	
5 - 2 ½" x WOF strips	F
Backing - 2 ⅝ yards	

LAP Cutting Instructions:

Background & Borders - 3 yards	
8 - 10" x WOF strips, subcut into: 32 - 10" squares	A

8 - 2 ½" x WOF strips, sew end to end and subcut into:
   2 - 2 ½" x 72 ½" strips
   2 - 2 ½" x 76 ½" strips
	B
	C

Blocks - One Layer Cake (32 - 10" squares)	
From 24 - 10" squares: 1 - 10" square (24 total)	D
From 8 - 10" squares: 1 - 10" square (8 total)	E
Binding - ⅞ yard	
9 - 2 ½" x WOF strips	F
Backing - 7 ¼ yards	

Good Times Blocks:

Each Good Times Block uses color coordinating fabric

Draw a diagonal line on the wrong side of the Fabric A squares.

With right sides facing, layer a Fabric A square with a Fabric D square.

Stitch ¼" from each side of the drawn line.

Cut apart on the marked line.

TRIM Outer Half Square Triangle Unit to measure:
   TABLE TOPPER - 4 ½" x 4 ½"
   LAP - 9 ½" x 9 ½"

Make forty-eight.

Assemble Block using coordinating fabric. Press open

Good Times Block should measure:
   TABLE TOPPER - 8 ½" x 8 ½"
   LAP - 18 ½" x 18 ½"

Make twelve.

With right sides facing, layer a Fabric A square with a Fabric E square.

Stitch ¼" from each side of the drawn line.

Cut apart on the marked line.

TRIM Inner Half Square Triangle Unit to measure:
   TABLE TOPPER - 4 ½" x 4 ½"
   LAP - 9 ½" x 9 ½"

Make sixteen.

ssemble Block using coordinating fabric. Press open.

enter Block should measure:

TABLE TOPPER - 8 ½" x 8 ½"
LAP - 18 ½" x 18 ½"

ake four.

uilt Assembly:

ssemble Quilt Center. Pay close attention to block
acement. Press rows open.

uilt Center should measure:

TABLE TOPPER - 32 ½" x 32 ½"
LAP - 72 ½" x 72 ½"

tach side borders using the Fabric B strips.

tach top and bottom borders using the Fabric C strips.

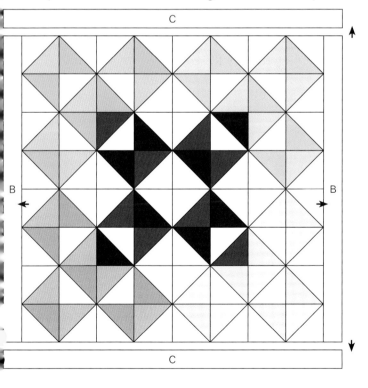

Another Idea:
At Home collection from
Bonnie & Camille

Another Idea:
Shine On collection by
Bonnie & Camille

nishing:

ece the Fabric F strips end to end for binding.

ilt and bind as desired.

Little Snippets Thread Catcher

Made by Bonnie Olaveson

Fabrics from *At Home* by Bonnie & Camille for Moda Fabrics

Little Snippets Thread Catcher

I love making little sewing projects, and this thread catcher is one of my favorites. Choose any quilt block for the outside and store all your extra threads and little snippets on the inside. This thread catcher really comes in handy when you are cutting out a quilt or sewing with friends. It has a special place for all the notions you want to keep close by and is the perfect addition to any retreat or quilt day sewing. Wouldn't it be fun to gift to your quilting friends, sewn with all their favorite quilt blocks?

— Bonnie

Little Snippets Thread Catcher

Cutting Instructions:

Block Background - Fat Eighth

1 - 2 ¾" x 21" strip, subcut into:	
2 - 2 ¾" squares	A
1 - 2" x 21" strip, subcut into:	
8 - 2" squares	B
1 - 1" x 21" strip, subcut into:	
10 - 1" squares	C

Block and Thread Catcher Bottom - Fat Quarter

1 - 5" x 21" strip, subcut into:	
1 - 5" x 6 ½" rectangle	D
1 - 2 ¾" x 21" strip, subcut into:	
4 - 2 ¾" squares	E
from the remainder of strip cut:	
8 - 1" squares	F

Block and Lining - Fat Quarter

2 - 6 ½" x 21" strips, subcut into:	
2 - 6 ½" squares	G
5 - 5" x 6 ½" rectangles	H
1 - 2 ¾" x 21" strip, subcut into:	
2 - 2 ¾" squares	I

Borders and Pockets - Fat Quarter

1 - 5" x 21" strip, subcut into:	
4 - 4" x 5" rectangles	J
3 - 1 ¼" x 21" strips, subcut into:	
4 - 1 ¼" x 6 ½" rectangles	K
4 - 1 ¼" x 5" rectangles	L

Binding - Fat Quarter

3 - 2 ½" x 21" strips, subcut into:	
2 - 2 ½" x 21" strips	M
2 - 2 ½" x 5" rectangles	N

Muslin - Fat Quarter

1 - 7" x 21" strip, subcut into:
2 - 7" squares
1 - 6 ½" x 21" strip, subcut into:
3 - 5" x 6 ½" rectangles

Batting - craft size

- 2 - 7" squares
- 3 - 5" x 6 ½" rectangles
- 2 - 4" x 5" rectangles

½" Ribbon

- 1 - 5" piece

Mix it up!

You can customize your thread catcher by using any of your favorite 4 ½" square blocks to make it your own. You would just need to make the borders a little larger. Or you can take off the borders and use a 6 ½" square block.

tar Blocks:

t the Fabric A squares, Fabric E squares and Fabric I
uares on the diagonal twice.

Make eight.   Make sixteen.   Make eight.

semble Unit. Press open.

urglass Unit should measure 2" x 2".

ke eight.

semble Unit. Press open.

nter Unit should measure 2" x 2".

ke two.

semble Block.

ar Block should measure 5" x 5".

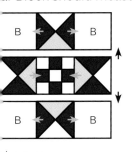   

ke two.

Borders:

Attach side borders using the Fabric L rectangles.

Attach top and bottom borders using the Fabric K rectangles.

Make two.

Quilted Star Blocks:

Layer one Star Block, one 7" Batting square and one 7" Muslin square.

Quilt as desired. Trim excess Batting and Muslin.

Baste ⅛" around the inside of the Quilted Star Block.

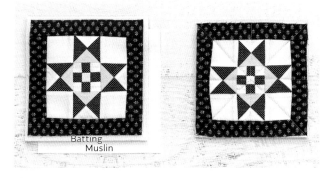

Make two.

Little Snippets Thread Catcher

Quilted Side Panels:

Layer one Fabric H rectangle, one 5" x 6 ½" Batting rectangle and one 5" x 6 ½" Muslin rectangle.

Quilt as desired.

Baste ⅛" around the inside of the Quilted Side Panels.

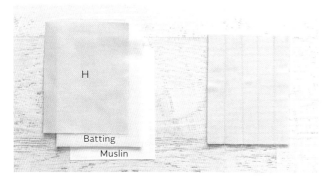

Make two.

Using matching thread, pin the 5" ribbon piece 2" from the top of one Quilted Side Panel edge.

Stitch the ribbon 2" from the left and right edges of one Quilted Side Panel.

This will create slots to put scissors, rulers and other sewing notions.

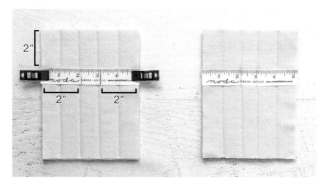

Make one.

Quilted Pockets:

Layer two Fabric J rectangles and one 4" x 5" Batting rectangle.

Quilt as desired.

Baste ⅛" around the inside of the Quilted Pocket.

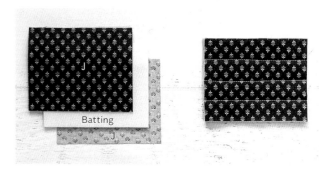

Make two.

With right sides facing, fold one Fabric N rectangle in half lengthwise. Press.

Attach the binding strip to the top edge of a Quilted Pocket.

Pull the binding around to the back and clip in place.

Finish with either machine or hand stitching.

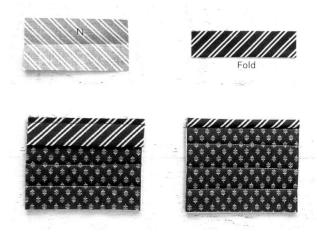

Make two.

one Quilted Pocket to one Quilted Side Panel,
atching the bottom raw edge.

tch ⅛" around the left, bottom and right edge of the
uilted Pocket to create a Finished Side Pocket.

ake one Ribbon Finished Side Pocket.
ake one Plain Finished Side Pocket.

uilted Thread Catcher Bottom:

yer the Fabric D rectangle, one 5" x 6 ½" Batting
ctangle and one 5" x 6 ½" Muslin rectangle.

uilt as desired.

ste ⅛" around the inside of the Quilted Thread
tcher Bottom.

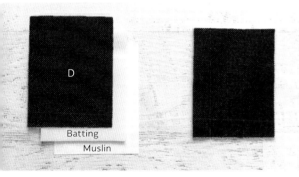

ke one.

Outer Thread Catcher Assembly:

Using a ¼" seam, stitch one Finished Side Pocket to
the right edge of one Quilted Star Block stopping ¼"
from the bottom.

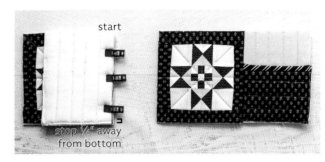

Make two Partial Top Outer Thread Catchers.

Using a ¼" seam, assemble the Top Outer Thread
Catcher stopping ¼" from the bottom.

Make one Top Outer Thread Catcher.

Little Snippets Thread Catcher

Using a ¼" seam, attach the Quilted Thread Catcher Bottom to the Top Outer Thread Catcher.

Turn right sides out.

Make one.

Lining Assembly:

Using a ¼" seam, stitch one Fabric G square to the right edge of one Fabric H rectangle stopping ¼" from the bottom.

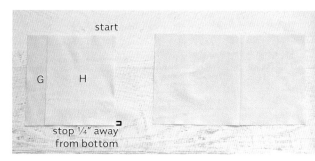

Make two Partial Top Lining Units.

Using a ¼" seam, assemble the Top Lining Unit stopping ¼" from the bottom.

Make one Top Lining Unit.

sing a ¼" seam, attach the remaining Fabric H
ctangle to the Top Lining Unit.

peat the same steps as the Outer Thread Catcher.

Piece the Fabric M strips end to end for binding.

Attach the Fabric M binding strip to the top edge of the Thread Catcher.

Pull the binding around to the inside and clip in place.

Finish with either machine or hand stitching.

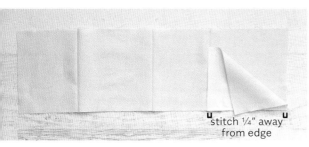

stitch ¼" away
from edge

ake one.

hread Catcher Assembly:

th wrong sides together, place the Lining Unit inside
e Outer Thread Catcher. Pin raw edges in place.

ing an ⅛" seam, stitch along top edges to secure.

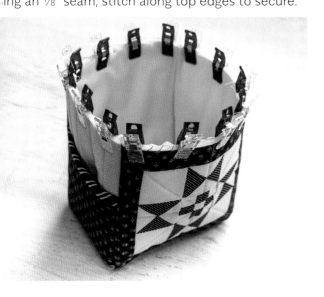

The Bonnie & Camille   73   Quilt Bee

Shine On Sampler Quilt

Pieced by Kimberly Jolly and Binding by Deborah Hawkins
Quilted by Nicole Christoffersen
Fabrics from Shine On by Bonnie & Camille for Moda Fabrics

Shine On Sampler Quilt

We share a love of sampler quilts, and when we started working on this book, this was the very first thing we designed. The Shine On Sampler uses many of our very favorite quilt blocks, and all of the quilts in this book were inspired by the blocks used in this quilt. After all, one of the best things about sampler quilts is you get to "sample" a block by just making one or two and if you love making it and want to make a whole quilt, you can do that too! This quilt is made from our Shine On collection for Moda and we couldn't love it more, but it could also be made from your scrap bin, all solids, all reds or navys, with a darker background, etc. The sky is the limit! We can't wait to see what you come up with!

— Bonnie & Camille

Shine On Sampler

68 ½" x 80 ½"

Block of the Month Breakdown

Month 1	Month 2	Month 3
Beehive Block (page 78)	Bloom Block (page 84)	Checkerboard Block (page 90)
Bee's Knees Block (page 79)	Butterfly Block (page 87)	Cheerful Block (page 92)
Bliss Block (page 83)	Celebrate Block (page 88)	Criss Cross Block (page 94)
Month 4	**Month 5**	**Month 6**
Cross Stitch Block (page 96)	Double Star Block (page 98)	Evening Star Block (page 103)
	Dream Block (page 100)	
	Eight Point Star Block (page 102)	
Month 7	**Month 8**	**Month 9**
Flutter Block (page 104)	Home Again Block (page 110)	Nine Patch Block (page 116)
Friendship Star Block (page 105)	Lighthearted Block (page 112)	Plaid Block (page 117)
Good Times Block (page 106)	Neighborhood Block (page 114)	
Happy Day Block (page 108)		
Month 10	**Month 11**	**Month 12**
Rainbow Block (page 119)	Starburst Block (page 124)	Sampler Finishing (page 130)
Sparkling Star Block (page 121)	Summer Block (page 126)	
Spring Block (page 123)	Sunshine Block (page 128)	

Quilt Kit Fabric Requirements

...st below includes fabric requirements to make the entire quilt, if you want to sew as a quilt kit. Fabric requirements for each block are listed in the individual block pages, if you want to sew as a block of the month.

· Quilt features the Shine On fabric collection by Bonnie & Camille for Moda Fabrics.

55210-11
Blocks
10" square

55210-12
Blocks
½ yard

55210-14
Blocks
⅞ yard

55210-16
Blocks
⅓ yard

55210-17
Blocks
⅓ yard

55211-11
Blocks
⅓ yard

55211-13
Blocks
Fat Eighth

55211-17
Blocks
⅓ yard

55211-20
Blocks
¼ yard

55212-11
Blocks
⅓ yard

55212-12
Blocks
⅝ yard

55212-16
Blocks
⅜ yard

55212-17
Blocks
¾ yard

55212-19
Blocks
⅓ yard

55213-13
Blocks
¼ yard

55214-11
Blocks
⅔ yard

55214-17
Blocks
⅜ yard

55214-20
Blocks
Fat Eighth

55215-11
Blocks
⅓ yard

55215-13
Blocks
½ yard

55215-15
Blocks
½ yard

55215-17
Blocks
⅔ yard

55215-18
Blocks
⅓ yard

55216-13
Blocks
¼ yard

55216-15
Blocks
½ yard

55216-18
Blocks
½ yard

55217-16
Blocks
⅝ yard

55217-19
Blocks
⅜ yard

55218-11
Blocks
1 yard

55218-12
Blocks
1 ½ yards

55218-14
Blocks
⅝ yard

55218-16
Blocks
⅞ yard

55218-17
Blocks
⅝ yard

55218-21
Background
6 yards

55215-17
Binding
⅞ yard

55210-17
Backing
5 ⅛ yards

Beehive Block

8 ½" x 8 ½"
Make one

Cutting Instructions:

Background - Fat Eighth		
	1 – 3" x 21" strip, subcut into: 4 – 3" squares	A
	1 – 2 ½" x 21" strip, subcut into: 4 – 2 ½" squares	B
Block - Four 10" squares		
	From each 10" square cut: 1 – 3" square	C
Block - Four 10" squares		
	From each 10" square cut: 1 – 2 ½" square	D

Piecing Instructions:

Each Corner Unit uses two coordinating 10" squares (set).

Draw a diagonal line on the wrong side of the Fabric A squares.

With right sides facing, layer a Fabric A square with a Fabric C square.

Stitch ¼" from each side of the drawn line.

Cut apart on the marked line.

TRIM Half Square Triangle Unit to measure 2 ½" x 2 ½".

Make two from each print.
Make eight total.

Assemble Unit using coordinating fabric. Press open.
Corner Unit should measure 4 ½" x 4 ½".

Make one from each set.
Make four total.

Assemble Block. Press open.

Beehive Block should measure 8 ½" x 8 ½".

Make one.

Bee's Knees Block

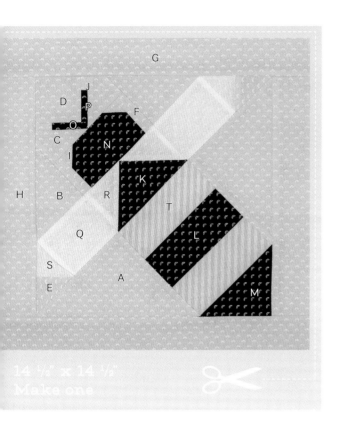

14 ½" x 14 ½"
Make one

Cutting Instructions:

Background - ½ yard

1 - 8 ¾" x WOF strip, subcut into:
   1 - 8 ¾" square   A
from remainder of strip cut:
   1 - 5 ½" square   B
   1 - 3 ¼" square   C
   1 - 2 ⅝" square   D
   1 - 2 ½" square   E
   2 - 1" x 2 ½" rectangles   F

2 - 2 ¼" x WOF strips, subcut into:
   2 - 2 ¼" x 14 ¾" rectangles   G
   2 - 2 ¼" x 11 ¼" rectangles   H
from remainder of strip cut:
   2 - 1 ¼" squares   I
   2 - ¾" x 1 ¼" rectangles   J

Block - Fat Eighth

1 - 5" x 21" strip, subcut into:
   1 - 2 ¾" x 5" rectangle   K
   1 - 2 ¼" x 5" rectangle   L
from remainder of strip cut:
   1 - 4 ⅛" square   M
   1 - 2 ½" x 4" rectangle   N
   1 - ¾" x 2 ⅛" rectangle   O
   1 - ¾" x 1 ⅞" rectangle   P

Block - Fat Eighth

1 - 2 ¾" x 21" strip, subcut into:
   2 - 2 ¾" x 3 ½" rectangles   Q
   2 - 2 ¾" squares   R
from remainder of strip cut:
   1 - 2 ½" square   S

Block - 10" square

From the 10" square cut:
   2 - 2 ¼" x 5" rectangles   T

Bee's Knees Block

Piecing Instructions:

Cut the Fabric A square and Fabric B square on the diagonal twice.

Make four.   Make four.

Cut the Fabric C square, Fabric E square, Fabric M square and Fabric S square on the diagonal once.

Make two.   Make two.

Make two.   Make two.

Assemble Unit. Press open.

Partial Antennae Unit should measure 2 ⅝" x 2 ⅞".

Make one.

Assemble Unit. Press open.

Antennae Unit should measure 2 ⅞" x 2 ⅞".

Make one.

Assemble Partial Top Bee Unit. Press open.

Make one.

Draw a diagonal line on the wrong side of the Fabric I squares.

With right sides facing, layer a Fabric I square on the top left corner of the Fabric N rectangle.

Stitch on the drawn line and trim ¼" away from the seam.

Repeat on the top right corner.

Partial Bee Head Unit should measure 2 ½" x 4".

Make one.

Assemble Unit. Press open.

Bee Head Unit should measure 2 ½" x 5".

Make one.

Draw a diagonal line on the wrong side of the Fabric R squares.

With right sides facing, layer a Fabric R square on one end of the Fabric K rectangle.

Stitch on the drawn line and trim ¼" away from the seam.

Repeat on the opposite end.

Flying Geese Unit should measure 2 ¾" x 5".

Make one.

Assemble Top Bee Unit. Press open.

TRIM the left and right edge.

Make one.

semble Partial Left Bee Wing Unit.

ake one.

semble Left Bee Wing Unit. Press open.

ake one.

semble Partial Right Bee Wing Unit.

ake one.

semble Right Bee Wing Unit. Press open.

ake one.
u will not use all Fabric B triangles.

semble Top Bee Body Unit.

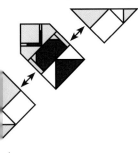 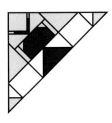

ake one.

Assemble Bottom Bee Body Unit.

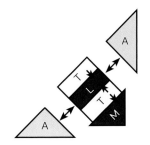 

Make one.
You will not use all Fabric A and Fabric M triangles.

Assemble Unit.
Bee's Knees Unit should measure 11 ¼" x 11 ¼".

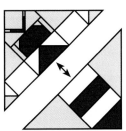 

Make one.

Assemble Block. Press open.
TRIM Bee's Knees Block to measure 14 ½" x 14 ½".

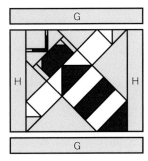 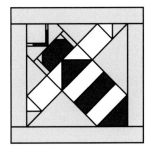

Make one.

Bliss Block

10 ½" x 10 ½"
Make one

Cutting Instructions:

Background - 10" square		
From the 10" square cut: 5 - 2 ½" squares		A

Block - Fat Eighth		
2 - 2 ½" x 21" strips, subcut into: 4 - 2 ½" x 4 ½" rectangles 4 - 2 ½" squares		B C

Block - 10" square		
From the 10" square cut: 4 - 2 ½" x 4 ½" rectangles		D

Piecing Instructions:

ssemble Unit.

orner Unit should measure 4 ½" x 4 ½".

ake four.

ssemble Block.

liss Block should measure 10 ½" x 10 ½".

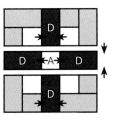 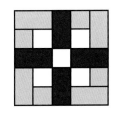

ake one.

Bloom Block

10 ½" x 20 ½"
Make one

Cutting Instructions:

Background - Fat Quarter

1 - 3 ¾" x 21" strip, subcut into:	
2 - 3 ¾" x 5" rectangles	A
2 - 2 ¾" x 3 ¾" rectangles	B
1 - 2" x 21" strip, subcut into:	
2 - 2" x 5" rectangles	C
4 - 2" squares	D
2 - 1 ½" x 21" strips, subcut into:	
2 - 1 ½" x 8 ¼" rectangles	E
14 - 1 ½" squares	F
1 - 1 ¼" x 21" strip, subcut into:	
2 - 1 ¼" x 4" rectangles	G

Block - 10" square

From the 10" square cut:	
1 - 3 ¾" x 6" rectangle	H

Block - 10" square

From the 10" square cut:	
1 - 3 ¾" x 4 ¾" rectangle	I

Block - 10" square

From the 10" square cut:	
1 - 4" x 4 ¾" rectangle	J

Block - 10" square

From the 10" square cut:	
1 - 3 ¾" x 4 ¾" rectangle	K

Block - Fat Eighth

1 - 4 ½" x 21" strip, subcut into:	
2 - 4 ½" squares	L
1 - 1 ½" x 21" strip, subcut into:	
1 - 1 ½" x 13" rectangle	M

Block - 10" square

From the 10" square cut:	
2 - 4 ½" squares	N

Piecing Instructions:

Draw a diagonal line on the wrong side of the Fabric D squares.

With right sides facing, layer a Fabric D square on the top left corner of the Fabric H rectangle.

Stitch on the drawn line and trim ¼" away from the seam.

Repeat on the top right corner.

Partial Top Bloom Unit should measure 3 ¾" x 6".

Make one.

Assemble Unit.

Top Bloom Unit should measure 3 ¾" x 10 ½".

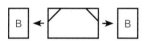 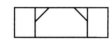

Make one.

Draw a diagonal line on the wrong side of the Fabric F squares.

With right sides facing, layer a Fabric D square on the top left corner of the Fabric I rectangle.

Stitch on the drawn line and trim ¼" away from the seam.

Repeat on the bottom left and bottom right corners with Fabric F squares.

Left Bloom Unit should measure 3 ¾" x 4 ¾".

Make one.

With right sides facing, layer a Fabric F square on the bottom left corner of the Fabric J rectangle.

Stitch on the drawn line and trim ¼" away from the seam.

Repeat on the bottom right corner.

Middle Bloom Unit should measure 4" x 4 ¾".

Make one.

With right sides facing, layer a Fabric D square on the top right corner of the Fabric K rectangle.

Stitch on the drawn line and trim ¼" away from the seam.

Repeat on the bottom left and bottom right corners with Fabric F squares.

Right Bloom Unit should measure 3 ¾" x 4 ¾".

Make one.

Assemble Unit. Press open.

Bottom Bloom Unit should measure 4 ¾" x 10 ½".

Make one.

Bloom Block

Draw a diagonal line on the wrong side of the Fabric N squares.

With right sides facing, layer a Fabric N square with a Fabric L square.

Stitch ¼" from each side of the drawn line.

Cut apart on the marked line.

TRIM Half Square Triangle Unit to measure 4" x 4".

Make four.

With right sides facing, layer a Fabric F square on the top right corner of a Half Square Triangle Unit.

Stitch on the drawn line and trim ¼" away from the seam.

Repeat on the bottom left corner.

Partial Leaf Unit should measure 4" x 4".

Make four.

Assemble Unit.

Left Leaf Unit should measure 5" x 8 ¼".

Make one.

Assemble Unit.

Right Leaf Unit should measure 5" x 8 ¼".

Make one.

Assemble Unit.

Leaf Unit should measure 10 ½" x 13".

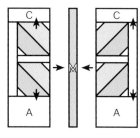 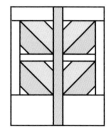

Make one.

Assemble Block. Press open.

Bloom Block should measure 10 ½" x 20 ½".

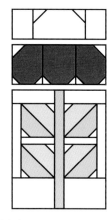 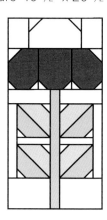

Make one.

Butterfly Block

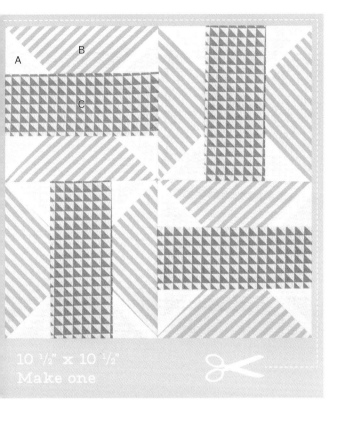

10 ½" x 10 ½"
Make one

Cutting Instructions:

Background - Fat Eighth		
2 - 2" x 21" strips, subcut into:		
16 - 2" squares		A

Block - Fat Eighth		
3 - 2" x 21" strips, subcut into:		
8 - 2" x 5 ½" rectangles		B

Block - Fat Eighth		
1 - 5 ½" x 21" strip, subcut into:		
4 - 2 ½" x 5 ½" rectangles		C

Piecing Instructions:

Draw a diagonal line on the wrong side of the Fabric A squares.

With right sides facing, layer a Fabric A square on the left end of a Fabric B rectangle.

Stitch on the drawn line and trim ¼" away from the seam.

Repeat on the right end.

Butterfly Wing Unit should measure 2" x 5 ½".

Make eight.

Assemble Unit. Press open.

Butterfly Unit should measure 5 ½" x 5 ½".

Make four.

Assemble Block. Press open.

Butterfly Block should measure 10 ½" x 10 ½".

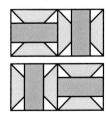 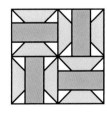

Make one.

Celebrate Block

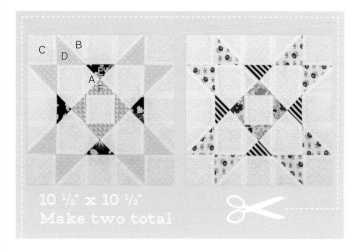

10 ½" x 10 ½"
Make two total

Cutting Instructions:

Background – ⅜ yard		
1 - 3 ¼" x WOF strip, subcut into:		
4 - 3 ¼" squares		A
from remainder of strip cut:		
8 - 3" squares		B
2 - 2 ½" x WOF strips, subcut into:		
26 - 2 ½" squares		C

Block - Two 10" squares		
From each 10" square cut:		
4 - 3" squares		D

Block - Two 10" squares		
From each 10" square cut:		
1 - 3 ¼" square		E

Block - Two 10" squares		
From each 10" square cut:		
1 - 3 ¼" square		F

Piecing Instructions:

Each Celebrate Block uses three 10" squares (set).

Draw a diagonal line on the wrong side of the Fabric B squares.

With right sides facing, layer a Fabric B square with a Fabric D square.

Stitch ¼" from each side of the drawn line.

Cut apart on the marked line.

TRIM Half Square Triangle Unit to measure 2 ½" x 2 ½".

Make eight from each print.
Make sixteen total.

Assemble Unit using matching fabric. Press open.

Corner Unit should measure 4 ½" x 4 ½".

Make four from each print.
Make eight total.

Cut the Fabric A squares, Fabric E squares and Fabric F squares on the diagonal twice.

Make sixteen.

Make four from each print.
Make eight total.

Make four from each print.
Make eight total.

Assemble Unit using coordinating fabric. Press open.

Hourglass Unit should measure 2 ½" x 2 ½".

Make four from each print.
Make eight total.

Assemble Unit. Press open.

Middle Unit should measure 2 ½" x 4 ½".

Make four from each print.
Make eight total.

Assemble Block using coordinating fabric. Press open.

Celebrate Block should measure 10 ½" x 10 ½".

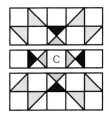 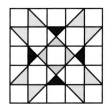

Make two total.

Checkerboard Block

12 ½" x 12 ½"
Make one

Cutting Instructions:

Block - 10" square		
	From the 10" square cut: 1 - 2 ½" square	A
Block - 10" square		
	From the 10" square cut: 2 - 2 ½" squares	B
Block - 10" square		
	From the 10" square cut: 3 - 2 ½" squares	C
Block - 10" square		
	From the 10" square cut: 4 - 2 ½" squares	D
Block - 10" square		
	From the 10" square cut: 5 - 2 ½" squares	E
Block - 10" square		
	From the 10" square cut: 6 - 2 ½" squares	F
Block - 10" square		
	From the 10" square cut: 5 - 2 ½" squares	G
Block - 10" square		
	From the 10" square cut: 4 - 2 ½" squares	H
Block - 10" square		
	From the 10" square cut: 3 - 2 ½" squares	I
Block - 10" square		
	From the 10" square cut: 2 - 2 ½" squares	J
Block - 10" square		
	From the 10" square cut: 1 - 2 ½" square	K

Piecing Instructions:

Assemble Block. Press open.

Checkerboard Block should measure 12 ½" x 12 ½".

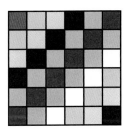

Make one.

Cheerful Block

10 ½" x 10 ½"
Make one

Cutting Instructions:

Background - Fat Quarter	
3 - 3" x 21" strips, subcut into: 16 - 3" squares	A

Block - Fat Eighth	
1 - 5 ½" x 21" strip, subcut into: 4 - 3" x 5 ½" rectangles	B

Block - Fat Eighth	
1 - 5 ½" x 21" strip, subcut into: 4 - 3" x 5 ½" rectangles	C

Piecing Instructions:

Draw a diagonal line on the wrong side of the Fabric A squares.

With right sides facing, layer a Fabric A square on the top end of a Fabric B rectangle.

Stitch on the drawn line and trim ¼" away from the seam.

Repeat on the bottom end.

Navy Flying Geese Unit should measure 3" x 5 ½".

Make four.

With right sides facing, layer a Fabric A square on the top end of a Fabric C rectangle.

Stitch on the drawn line and trim ¼" away from the seam.

Repeat on the bottom end.

Cherry Flying Geese Unit should measure 3" x 5 ½".

Make four.

Assemble Unit. Press open.

Cheerful Unit should measure 5 ½" x 5 ½".

Make four.

Assemble Block. Press open.

Cheerful Block should measure 10 ½" x 10 ½".

Make one.

Criss Cross Block

12 ½" x 12 ½"
Make one

Cutting Instructions:

Background - Fat Eighth	
1 - 4 ½" x 21" strip, subcut into: 4 - 4 ½" squares	A
1 - 2 ½" x 21" strip, subcut into: 8 - 2 ½" squares	B

Block - 10" square	
From the 10" square cut: 2 - 2 ½" squares	C

Block - 10" square	
From the 10" square cut: 2 - 2 ½" squares	D

Block - 10" square	
From the 10" square cut: 2 - 2 ½" squares	E

Block - 10" square	
From the 10" square cut: 2 - 2 ½" squares	F

Block - 10" square	
From the 10" square cut: 2 - 2 ½" squares	G

Block - 10" square	
From the 10" square cut: 2 - 2 ½" squares	H

iecing Instructions:

ssemble Unit.

orner One Four Patch Unit should measure
½" x 4 ½".

ake two.

ssemble Unit.

orner Two Four Patch Unit should measure
½" x 4 ½".

ake two.

ssemble Unit.

enter Four Patch Unit should measure 4 ½" x 4 ½".

ake one.

ssemble Block. Press open.

riss Cross Block should measure 12 ½" x 12 ½".

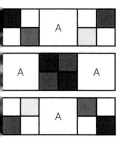   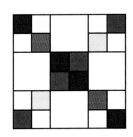

ake one.

Cross Stitch Block

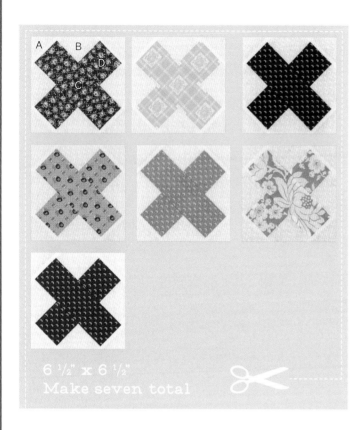

6 ½" x 6 ½"
Make seven total

Cutting Instructions:

Background - ½ yard		
5 - 2 ½" x WOF strips, subcut into:		
28 - 2 ½" x 3 ½" rectangles		A
28 - 2 ½" squares		B

Block - Seven 10" squares

From each 10" square cut:
1 - 2 ½" x 6 ½" rectangle   C
2 - 2 ½" squares   D

Piecing Instructions:

Assemble Unit using matching fabric.
Center Unit should measure 6 ½" x 6 ½".

Make one from each 10" square.
Make seven total.

Fold the Center Unit into quarters to create center creases.

Make seven total.

Fold the Fabric A rectangle in half to create a center crease.

Make twenty-eight.

Assemble Block matching center creases. Press open
TRIM Cross Stitch Block to measure 6 ½" x 6 ½".

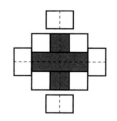 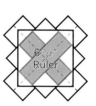

Make seven total.

Double Star Block

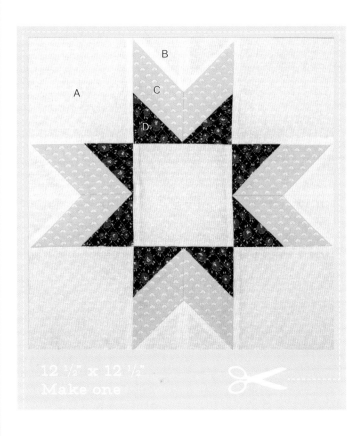

12 ½" x 12 ½"
Make one

Cutting Instructions:

Background - Fat Quarter	
2 - 4 ½" x 21" strips, subcut into: 5 - 4 ½" squares	A
1 - 2 ½" x 21" strip, subcut into: 8 - 2 ½" squares	B

Block - Fat Eighth		
	1 - 4 ½" x 21" strip, subcut into: 8 - 2 ½" x 4 ½" rectangles	C

Block - 10" square		
	From the 10" square cut: 8 - 2 ½" squares	D

Piecing Instructions:

Draw a diagonal line on the wrong side of the Fabric B squares and Fabric D squares.

With right sides facing, layer a Fabric B square on the top end of a Fabric C rectangle.

Stitch on the drawn line and trim ¼" away from the seam.

Repeat on the bottom end with a Fabric D square.

Left Star Point Unit should measure 2 ½" x 4 ½".

Make four.

With right sides facing, layer a Fabric B square on the top end of a Fabric C rectangle.

Stitch on the drawn line and trim ¼" away from the seam.

Repeat on the bottom end with a Fabric D square.

Right Star Point Unit should measure 2 ½" x 4 ½".

Make four.

ssemble Unit.

tar Point Unit should measure 4 ½" x 4 ½".

ake four.

Assemble Block. Press open.

Double Star Block should measure 12 ½" x 12 ½".

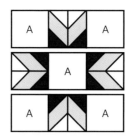 

Make one.

Dream Block

14 ½" x 14 ½"
Make one

Background - Fat Eighth

5 - 1 ½" x 21" strips, subcut into:
4 - 1 ½" x 6" rectangles	A
4 - 1 ½" x 5" rectangles	B
4 - 1 ½" x 3 ½" rectangles	C
4 - 1 ½" x 2 ½" rectangles	D

Block - Four 10" squares

From each 10" square cut:
1 - 2 ½" square	E

Block - Four 10" squares

From each 10" square cut:
1 - 2" x 5" rectangle	F
1 - 2" x 3 ½" rectangle	G

Block - Four 10" squares

From each 10" square cut:
1 - 2" x 7 ½" rectangle	H
1 - 2" x 6" rectangle	I

Piecing Instructions:

Each Dream Unit uses three 10" squares (set).

Assemble Unit using coordinating fabric.
Center Dream Unit should measure 3 ½" x 5".

Make one from each set.
Make four total.

Assemble Unit using coordinating fabric.
Partial Dream Unit should measure 6" x 7 ½".

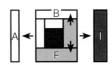

Make one from each set.
Make four total.

ssemble Unit using matching fabric.

ream Unit should measure 7 ½" x 7 ½".

ake one from each set.

ake four total.

Assemble Block.

Dream Block should measure 14 ½" x 14 ½".

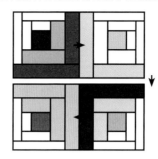 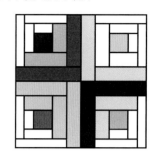

Make one.

Eight Point Star Block

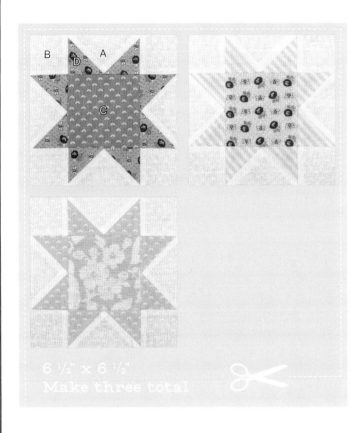

6 ½" x 6 ½"
Make three total

Cutting Instructions:

Background - Fat Quarter	
5 - 2" x 21" strips, subcut into:	
12 - 2" x 3 ½" rectangles	A
12 - 2" squares	B
Block - Three 10" squares	
From each 10" square cut:	
1 - 3 ½" square	C
Block - Three 10" squares	
From each 10" square cut:	
8 - 2" squares	D

Piecing Instructions:

Each Eight Point Star Block uses two 10" squares (set).

Draw a diagonal line on the wrong side of the Fabric D squares.

With right sides facing, layer a Fabric D square on one end of a Fabric A rectangle.

Stitch on the drawn line and trim ¼" away from the seam.

Repeat on the opposite end with matching fabric.

Flying Geese Unit should measure 2" x 3 ½".

Make four from each 10" square.
Make twelve total.

Assemble Block using coordinating fabric. Press open.

Eight Point Star Block should measure 6 ½" x 6 ½".

Make one from each set.
Make three total.

Evening Star Block

6 ½" x 6 ½"
Make four total

Cutting Instructions:

Background - Fat Quarter	
4 - 2" x 21" strips, subcut into: 32 - 2" squares	A

Block - Four 10" squares	
From each 10" square cut: 1 - 3 ½" square	B

Block - Four 10" squares	
From each 10" square cut: 4 - 2" x 3 ½" rectangles	C
4 - 2" squares	D

Piecing Instructions:

ach Evening Star Block uses two 10" squares (set).

raw a diagonal line on the wrong side of the Fabric A
quares.

ith right sides facing, layer a Fabric A square on one
d of a Fabric C rectangle.

itch on the drawn line and trim ¼" away from the
am.

peat on the opposite end.

ying Geese Unit should measure 2" x 3 ½".

ake four from each 10" square.
ake sixteen total.

Assemble Block using coordinating fabric. Press open.
Evening Star Block should measure 6 ½" x 6 ½".

Make one from each set.
Make four total.

Flutter Block

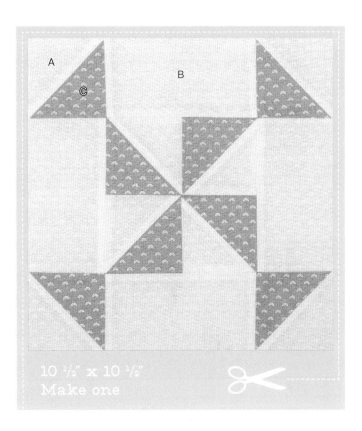

10 ½" x 10 ½"
Make one

Cutting Instructions:

Background - Fat Quarter		
	1 - 3 ½" x 21" strip, subcut into: 4 - 3 ½" squares	A
	1 - 5 ½" x 21" strip, subcut into: 4 - 3" x 5 ½" rectangles	B
Block - 10" square		
	From the 10" square cut: 4 - 3 ½" squares	C

Piecing Instructions:

Draw a diagonal line on the wrong side of the Fabric A squares.

With right sides facing, layer a Fabric A square with a Fabric C square.

Stitch ¼" from each side of the drawn line.

Cut apart on the marked line.

TRIM Half Square Triangle Unit to measure 3" x 3".

Make eight.

Assemble Unit.

Center Unit should measure 5 ½" x 5 ½".

Make one.

Assemble Block. Press open.

Flutter Block should measure 10 ½" x 10 ½".

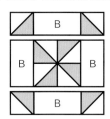 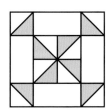

Make one.

Friendship Star Block

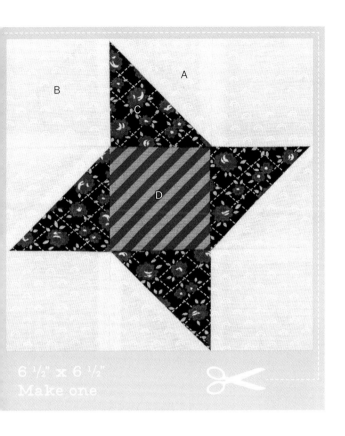

6 ½" x 6 ½"
Make one

Cutting Instructions:

Background - 10" square		
	From the 10" square cut:	
	2 - 3" squares	A
	4 - 2 ½" squares	B
Block - 10" square		
	From the 10" square cut:	
	2 - 3" squares	C
Block - 10" square		
	From the 10" square cut:	
	1 - 2 ½" square	D

Piecing Instructions:

Draw a diagonal line on the wrong side of the Fabric A squares.

With right sides facing, layer a Fabric A square with a Fabric C square.

Stitch ¼" from each side of the drawn line.

Cut apart on the marked line.

TRIM Half Square Triangle Unit to measure 2 ½" x 2 ½".

Make four.

Assemble Block. Press open.

Friendship Star Block should measure 6 ½" x 6 ½".

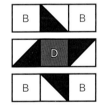 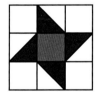

Make one.

Good Times Block

24 ½" x 24 ½"
Make one

Cutting Instructions:

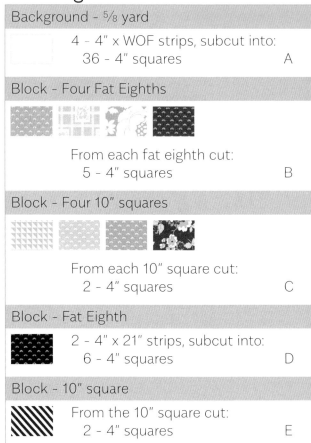

Background - ⅝ yard	
4 - 4" x WOF strips, subcut into: 36 - 4" squares	A
Block - Four Fat Eighths	
From each fat eighth cut: 5 - 4" squares	B
Block - Four 10" squares	
From each 10" square cut: 2 - 4" squares	C
Block - Fat Eighth	
2 - 4" x 21" strips, subcut into: 6 - 4" squares	D
Block - 10" square	
From the 10" square cut: 2 - 4" squares	E

Piecing Instructions:

Each Corner Unit uses one fat eighth and one 10" square (set).

Draw a diagonal line on the wrong side of the Fabric A squares.

With right sides facing, layer a Fabric A square with a Fabric B square.

Stitch ¼" from each side of the drawn line.

Cut apart on the marked line.

TRIM Outer Half Square Triangle Unit to measure 3 ½" x 3 ½".

Make ten from each fat eighth.
Make forty total.

With right sides facing, layer a Fabric A square with a Fabric C square.

Stitch ¼" from each side of the drawn line.

Cut apart on the marked line.

TRIM Inner Half Square Triangle Unit to measure 3 ½" x 3 ½".

Make four from each 10" square.
Make sixteen total.

ssemble Unit using coordinating fabric. Press open.

orner Unit should measure 6 ½" x 6 ½".

ake three from each set.

ake twelve total.

ou will not use all Half Square Triangle Units.

ith right sides facing, layer a Fabric A square with a

bric E square.

itch ¼" from each side of the drawn line.

ut apart on the marked line.

RIM Middle Half Square Triangle Unit to measure

½" x 3 ½".

ake four.

ith right sides facing, layer a Fabric A square with a

bric D square.

itch ¼" from each side of the drawn line.

ut apart on the marked line.

RIM Center Half Square Triangle Unit to measure

½" x 3 ½".

ake twelve.

Assemble Unit. Press open.

Center Unit should measure 6 ½" x 6 ½".

Make four.

Assemble Unit using coordinating fabric. Press open.

Good Times Unit should measure 12 ½" x 12 ½".

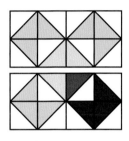   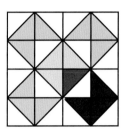

Make four.

Assemble Block. Press open.

Good Times Block should measure 24 ½" x 24 ½".

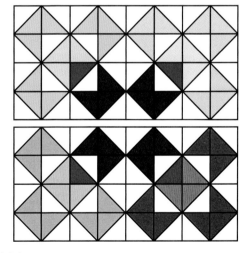

Make one.

Happy Day Block

16 ½" x 16 ½"
Make one

Cutting Instructions:

Background - Fat Eighth		
1 - 5" x 21" strip, subcut into:		
4 - 5" squares		A

Block - Fat Quarter		
1 - 5" x 21" strip, subcut into:		
2 - 5" squares		B
1 - 4 ½" x 21" strip, subcut into:		
4 - 4 ½" squares		C

Block - Fat Quarter		
1 - 5" x 21" strip, subcut into:		
2 - 5" squares		D
1 - 4 ½" x 21" strip, subcut into:		
4 - 4 ½" squares		E

Piecing Instructions:

Draw a diagonal line on the wrong side of the Fabric A squares.

With right sides facing, layer a Fabric A square with a Fabric B square.

Stitch ¼" from each side of the drawn line.

Cut apart on the marked line.

TRIM Dark Half Square Triangle Unit to measure 4 ½" x 4 ½".

Make four.

With right sides facing, layer a Fabric A square with a Fabric D square.

Stitch ¼" from each side of the drawn line.

Cut apart on the marked line.

TRIM Light Half Square Triangle Unit to measure 4 ½" x 4 ½".

Make four.

ssemble Unit. Press open.
uter One Unit should measure 8 ½" x 8 ½".

ake two.

ssemble Unit. Press open.
uter Two Unit should measure 8 ½" x 8 ½".

ake two.

Assemble Block. Press open.
Happy Day Block should measure 16 ½" x 16 ½".

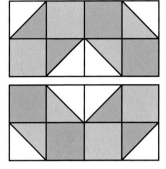 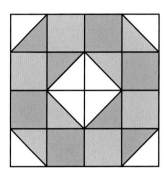

Make one.

Home Again Block

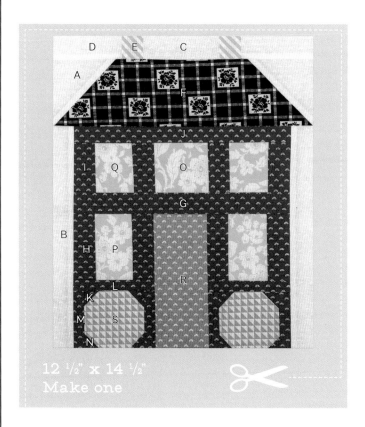

12 ½" x 14 ½"
Make one

Cutting Instructions:

Background - Fat Eighth

1 - 3 ½" x 21" strip, subcut into:		
	2 - 3 ½" squares	A
2 - 1 ½" x 21" strips, subcut into:		
	2 - 1 ½" x 10 ½" rectangles	B
	1 - 1 ½" x 4" rectangle	C
	2 - 1 ½" x 3 ¾" rectangles	D

Block - 10" square

From the 10" square cut:		
	2 - 1 ½" squares	E

Block - Fat Eighth

1 - 3 ½" x 21" strip, subcut into:		
	1 - 3 ½" x 12 ½" rectangle	F

Block - Fat Eighth

2 - 1 ½" x 21" strips, subcut into:		
	1 - 1 ½" x 10 ½" rectangle	G
	4 - 1 ½" x 3 ½" rectangles	H
	4 - 1 ½" x 2 ¾" rectangles	I
1 - 1 ¼" x 21" strip, subcut into:		
	1 - 1 ¼" x 10 ½" rectangle	J
	4 - 1 ¼" squares	K
2 - 1" x 21" strips, subcut into:		
	2 - 1" x 4 ¼" rectangles	L
	4 - 1" x 3" rectangles	M
	4 - 1" squares	N

Block - Fat Eighth

1 - 2 ¾" x 21" strip, subcut into:		
	1 - 2 ¾" x 3" rectangle	O
from remainder of strip cut:		
	2 - 2 ¼" x 3 ½" rectangles	P
	2 - 2 ¼" x 2 ¾" rectangles	Q

Block - 10" square

From the 10" square cut:		
	1 - 3" x 6 ½" rectangle	R

Block - 10" square

From the 10" square cut:		
	2 - 3" x 3 ¼" rectangles	S

Piecing Instructions:

Assemble Unit.

Chimney Unit should measure 1 ½" x 12 ½".

 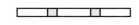

Make one.

Draw a diagonal line on the wrong side of the Fabric A squares.

With right sides facing, layer a Fabric A square on the left end of the Fabric F rectangle.

Stitch on the drawn line and trim ¼" away from the seam.

Repeat on the right end.

Roof Unit should measure 3 ½" x 12 ½".

Make one.

Assemble Unit.

Window Unit should measure 2 ¾" x 10 ½".

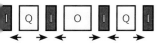 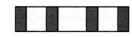

Make one.

Draw a diagonal line on the wrong side of the Fabric K squares and Fabric N squares.

With right sides facing, layer Fabric K squares on the top left and top right corners of a Fabric S rectangle.

Stitch on the drawn lines and trim ¼" away from the seam.

Repeat on the bottom left and bottom right corners with Fabric N squares.

Sash Unit should measure 3" x 3 ¼".

Make two.

Assemble Unit.

Outer Home Again Unit should measure 4 ¼" x 6 ½".

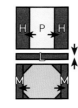 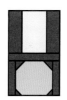

Make two.

Assemble Unit.

Bottom Home Again Unit should measure 6 ½" x 10 ½".

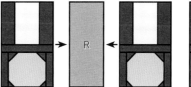 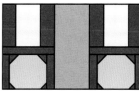

Make one.

Assemble Unit.

Home Again Unit should measure 10 ½" x 10 ½".

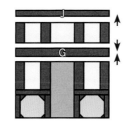 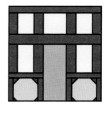

Make one.

Assemble Block.

Home Again Block should measure 12 ½" x 14 ½".

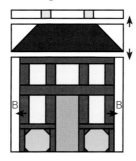 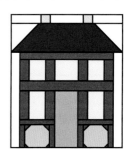

Make one.

Lighthearted Block

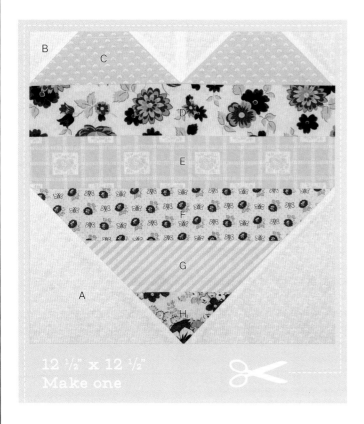

12 ½" x 12 ½"
Make one

Cutting Instructions:

Background - Fat Eighth		
1 - 6 ½" x 21" strip, subcut into:		
2 - 6 ½" squares		A
from remainder of strip cut:		
4 - 2 ½" squares		B

Block - 10" square		
From the 10" square cut:		
2 - 2 ½"x 6 ½" rectangles		C

Block - Fat Eighth		
1 - 2 ½" x 21" strip, subcut into:		
1 - 2 ½" x 12 ½" rectangle		D

Block - Fat Eighth		
1 - 2 ½" x 21" strip, subcut into:		
1 - 2 ½" x 12 ½" rectangle		E

Block - Fat Eighth		
1 - 2 ½" x 21" strip, subcut into:		
1 - 2 ½" x 12 ½" rectangle		F

Block - Fat Eighth		
1 - 2 ½" x 21" strip, subcut into:		
1 - 2 ½" x 12 ½" rectangle		G

Block - Fat Eighth		
1 - 2 ½" x 21" strip, subcut into:		
1 - 2 ½" x 12 ½" rectangle		H

Piecing Instructions:

Draw a diagonal line on the wrong side of the Fabric B squares.

With right sides facing, layer a Fabric B square on the left end of a Fabric C rectangle.

Stitch on the drawn line and trim ¼" away from the seam.

Repeat on the right end.

Top Lighthearted Unit should measure 2 ½" x 6 ½".

Make two.

Assemble Unit. Press open.

Lighthearted Unit should measure 12 ½" x 12 ½".

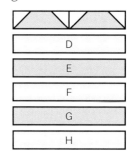   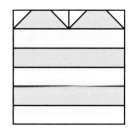

Make one.

aw a diagonal line on the wrong side of the Fabric A squares.

th right sides facing, layer a Fabric A square on the bottom left corner of the Lighthearted Unit.

tch on the drawn line and trim ¼" away from the seam.

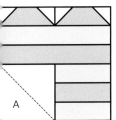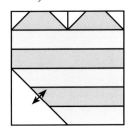

peat on the bottom right corner.

ghthearted Block should measure 12 ½" x 12 ½".

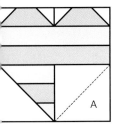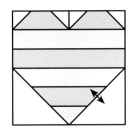

ke one.

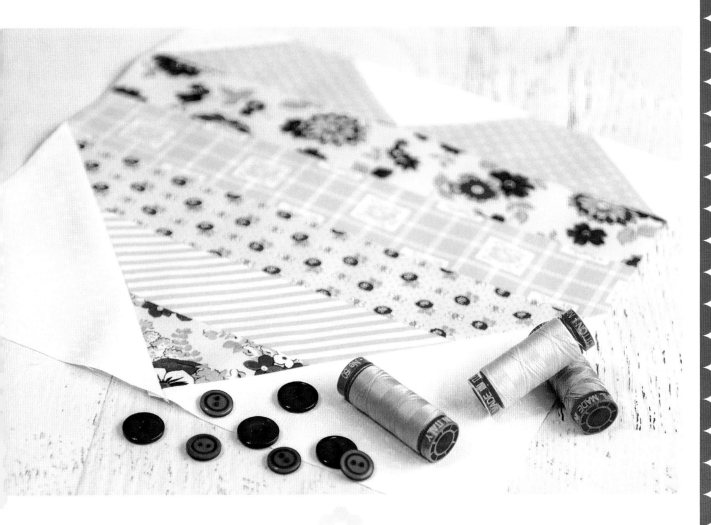

The Bonnie & Camille   113   Quilt Bee

Neighborhood Block

12 ½" x 12 ½"
Make one

Cutting Instructions:

Background - Fat Quarter		
1 - 4 ½" x 21" strip, subcut into:		
4 - 4 ½" squares		A
3 - 2 ½" x 21" strips, subcut into:		
4 - 2 ½" x 6 ½" rectangles		B
4 - 2 ½" x 4 ½" rectangles		C

Block - Four 10" squares		
From each 10" square cut:		
1 - 4 ½" square		D
3 - 2 ½" squares		E

Piecing Instructions:

Each Neighborhood Unit uses two 10" squares (set).

Draw a diagonal line on the wrong side of the Fabric A squares.

With right sides facing, layer a Fabric A square with a Fabric D square.

Stitch on the drawn line and trim ¼" away from the seam.

Half Square Triangle Unit should measure 4 ½" x 4 ½".

Make one from each 10" square.
Make four total.

Draw a diagonal line on the wrong side of the Fabric E squares.

With right sides facing, layer a Fabric E square on the top end of a Fabric C rectangle.

Stitch on the drawn line and trim ¼" away from the seam.

Right Neighborhood Unit should measure 2 ½" x 4 ½.

Make one from each 10" square.
Make four total.

th right sides facing, layer a Fabric E square on the
t end of a Fabric B rectangle.

tch on the drawn line and trim ¼" away from the
am.

peat on the right end with matching fabric.

ttom Neighborhood Unit should measure
½" x 6 ½".

ke one from each 10" square.
ke four total.

semble Unit using coordinating fabric. Press open.

ighborhood Unit should measure 6 ½" x 6 ½".

ke two from each set.
ke four total.

semble Block. Press open.

ighborhood Block should measure 12 ½" x 12 ½".

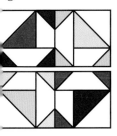 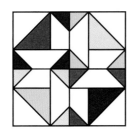

ke one.

Nine Patch Block

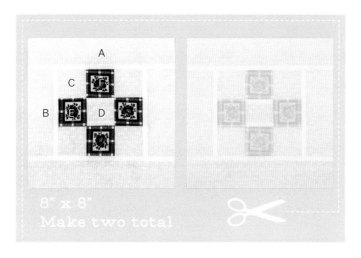

8" x 8"
Make two total

Cutting Instructions:

Background - Fat Quarter		
4 - 2" x 21" strips, subcut into:		
4 - 2" x 8" rectangles		A
4 - 2" x 5" rectangles		B
4 - 2" x 5" rectangles		C
2 - 2" squares		D

Block - Two 10" squares		
From each 10" square cut:		
1 - 2" x 5" rectangle		E
2 - 2" squares		F

Piecing Instructions:

Assemble two Fabric C rectangles and one Fabric E rectangle.

Strip Set should measure 5" x 5".

Make one from each 10" square.
Make two total.

Subcut each Strip Set into two 2" x 5" rectangles.

Outer Three Patch Unit should measure 2" x 5".

Make two from each 10" square.
Make four total.

Assemble two matching Fabric F squares and one Fabric D square.

Inner Three Patch Unit should measure 2" x 5".

Make one from each 10" square.
Make two total.

Assemble Unit using matching fabric.

Nine Patch Unit should measure 5" x 5".

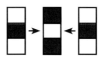

Make one from each 10" square.
Make two total.

Assemble Block. Press open.

Nine Patch Block should measure 8" x 8".

Make two total.

Plaid Block

8" x 8"
Make two total

Cutting Instructions:

Background - Fat Eighth		
	2 - 2" x 21" strips, subcut into:	
	2 - 2" x 9" rectangles	A
	2 - 2" squares	B

Block - Two 10" squares		
	From each 10" square cut:	
	1 - 2" x 9" rectangle	C

Block - Two 10" squares		
	From each 10" square cut:	
	2 - 2" x 9" rectangles	D

Block - Two 10" squares		
	From each 10" square cut:	
	1 - 2" x 9" rectangle	E

Block - Two 10" squares		
	From each 10" square cut:	
	1 - 2" x 9" rectangle	F

Plaid Block

Piecing Instructions:

Each Plaid Block uses four 10" squares (set).

Assemble one Fabric C rectangle and one coordinating Fabric D rectangle.

Strip Set One should measure 3 ½" x 9".

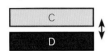 

Make one from each set.
Make two total.

Subcut each Strip Set One into four 2" x 3 ½" rectangles.

Two Patch Unit One should measure 2" x 3 ½".

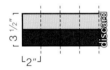

Make four from each set.
Make eight total.

Assemble one Fabric D rectangle and one coordinating Fabric E rectangle.

Strip Set Two should measure 3 ½" x 9".

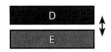 

Make one from each set.
Make two total.

Subcut each Strip Set Two into four 2" x 3 ½" rectangles.

Two Patch Unit Two should measure 2" x 3 ½".

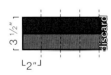

Make four from each set.
Make eight total.

Assemble one Fabric A rectangle and one Fabric F rectangle.

Strip Set Three should measure 3 ½" x 9".

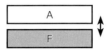 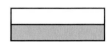

Make one from each set.
Make two total.

Subcut each Strip Set Three into four 2" x 3 ½" rectangles.

Two Patch Unit Three should measure 2" x 3 ½".

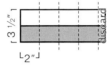

Make four from each set.
Make eight total.

Assemble Unit using coordinating fabric.

Four Patch Unit should measure 3 ½" x 3 ½".

Make four from each set.
Make eight total.

Assemble Block using coordinating fabric. Press open.

Plaid Block should measure 8" x 8".

Make one from each set.
Make two total.

Rainbow Block

B
C
E   F
H   I
D   K
G   J
A

6 ½" x 10 ½"
Make one

Cutting Instructions:

Background - 10" square		
From the 10" square cut:		
1 - 2 ¾" x 3" rectangle	A	
2 - 2 ¾" squares	B	

Block - Fat Eighth		
2 - 2" x 21" strips, subcut into:		
1 - 2" x 10 ½" rectangle	C	
2 - 2" x 5" rectangles	D	
2 - 2" squares	E	

Block - 10" square		
From the 10" square cut:		
1 - 1 ¾" x 7 ½" rectangle	F	
2 - 1 ¾" x 3 ¾" rectangles	G	
2 - 1 ¼" squares	H	

Block - 10" square		
From the 10" square cut:		
1 - 1 ½" x 5" rectangle	I	
2 - 1 ½" x 2 ¾" rectangles	J	
2 - 1" squares	K	

Piecing Instructions:

aw a diagonal line on the wrong side of the Fabric K
uares.

th right sides facing, layer a Fabric K square on the
o left corner of the Fabric A rectangle.

itch on the drawn line and trim ¼" away from the
am.

A

—3"—

peat on the top right corner.

nter Unit should measure 2 ¾" x 3".

ke one.

Assemble Unit.

Partial Bottom Rainbow Unit should measure 3 ¾" x 5".

J   J

Make one.

Rainbow Block

Draw a diagonal line on the wrong side of the Fabric H squares.

With right sides facing, layer a Fabric H square on the top left corner of the Partial Bottom Rainbow Unit.

Stitch on the drawn line and trim ¼" away from the seam.

Repeat on the top right corner.

Bottom Rainbow Unit should measure 3 ¾" x 5".

Make one.

Assemble Unit.

Partial Middle Rainbow Unit should measure 5" x 7 ½".

Make one.

Draw a diagonal line on the wrong side of the Fabric E squares.

With right sides facing, layer a Fabric E square on the top left corner of the Partial Middle Rainbow Unit.

Stitch on the drawn line and trim ¼" away from the seam.

Repeat on the top right corner.

Middle Rainbow Unit should measure 5" x 7 ½".

Make one.

Assemble Unit.

Partial Rainbow Unit should measure 6 ½" x 10 ½".

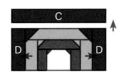 

Make one.

Draw a diagonal line on the wrong side of the Fabric B squares.

With right sides facing, layer a Fabric B square on the top left corner of the Partial Rainbow Unit.

Stitch on the drawn line and trim ¼" away from the seam.

Repeat on the top right corner.

Rainbow Block should measure 6 ½" x 10 ½".

Make one.

Sparkling Star Block

16 ½" x 16 ½"

Cutting Instructions:

Background - ½ yard		
1 - 4 ⅞" x WOF strip, subcut into:		
6 - 4 ⅞" squares		A
1 - 4 ½" x WOF strip, subcut into:		
4 - 4 ½" squares		B
1 - 2 ½" x WOF strip, subcut into:		
12 - 2 ½" squares		C

2 3/4

Block - Twelve 10" squares		

From each 10" square cut:
1 - 2 ⅞" square   D
1 - 2 ½" square   E

2 3/4

Piecing Instructions:

Draw a diagonal line on the wrong side of the Fabric C squares.

With right sides facing, layer a Fabric C square with a Fabric E square.

Stitch on the drawn line and trim ¼" away from the seam.

Half Square Triangle Unit should measure 2 ½" x 2 ½".

Make one from each 10" square.
Make twelve total.

Cut the Fabric A squares and Fabric D squares on the diagonal once.

Make twelve.

Make two from each 10" square.
Make twenty-four total.

Sparkling Star Block

Assemble Unit using matching fabric. Press open.
Sparkling Star Unit should measure 4 ½" x 4 ½".

Make one from each 10" square.
Make twelve total.

Assemble Block. Press open.
Sparkling Star Block should measure 16 ½" x 16 ½".

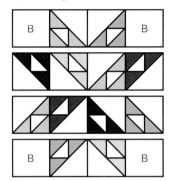 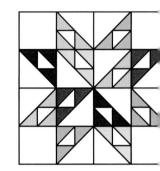

Make one.

Spring Block

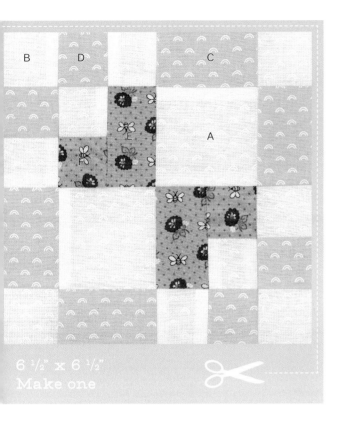

6 ½" x 6 ½"
Make one

Cutting Instructions:

Background - 10" square		
	From the 10" square cut:	
	2 - 2 ½" squares	A
	10 - 1 ½" squares	B
Block - 10" square		
	From the 10" square cut:	
	4 - 1 ½" x 2 ½" rectangles	C
	4 - 1 ½" squares	D
Block - 10" square		
	From the 10" square cut:	
	2 - 1 ½" x 2 ½" rectangles	E
	2 - 1 ½" squares	F

Piecing Instructions:

Assemble Unit.

Four Patch Unit should measure 2 ½" x 2 ½".

Make two.

Assemble Unit.

Spring One Unit should measure 3 ½" x 3 ½".

Make two.

Assemble Unit.

Spring Two Unit should measure 3 ½" x 3 ½".

Make two.

Assemble Block.

Spring Block should measure 6 ½" x 6 ½".

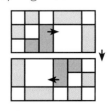

Make one.

Starburst Block

12 ½" x 12 ½"
Make one

Cutting Instructions:

Background - Fat Quarter		
1 - 3 ½" x 21" strip, subcut into:		
4 - 3 ½" squares		A
1 - 2 ½" x 21" strip, subcut into:		
4 - 2 ½" squares		B
2 - 2" x 21" strips, subcut into:		
8 - 2" x 5" rectangles		C

Block - Fat Eighth		
1 - 3 ½" x 21" strip, subcut into:		
1 - 3 ½" square		D
from remainder of strip cut:		
4 - 2 ½" squares		E
2 - 2" x 21" strips, subcut into:		
12 - 2" squares		F
8 - 2" squares		G

Piecing Instructions:

Draw a diagonal line on the wrong side of the Fabric B squares.

With right sides facing, layer a Fabric B square with a Fabric E square.

Stitch ¼" from each side of the drawn line.

Cut apart on the marked line.

TRIM Half Square Triangle Unit to measure 2" x 2".

Make eight.

Assemble Unit. Press open.

Partial Inner Unit should measure 3 ½" x 3 ½".

Make four.

Assemble Unit. Press open.

Inner Unit should measure 9 ½" x 9 ½".

 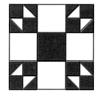

Make one.

Draw a diagonal line on the wrong side of the Fabric G squares.

With right sides facing, layer a Fabric G square on the right end of a Fabric C rectangle.

Stitch on the drawn line and trim ¼" away from the seam.

Left Unit should measure 2" x 5".

Make four.

With right sides facing, layer a Fabric G square on the left end of a Fabric C rectangle.

Stitch on the drawn line and trim ¼" away from the seam.

Right Unit should measure 2" x 5".

Make four.

Assemble Unit.

Outer Unit should measure 2" x 9 ½".

Make four.

Assemble Block. Press open.

Starburst Block should measure 12 ½" x 12 ½".

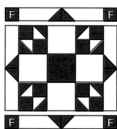 

Make one.

Summer Block

12 ½" x 12 ½"
Make one

Cutting Instructions:

Background - Fat Quarter	
1 - 5 ¼" x 21" strip, subcut into:	
1 - 5 ¼" square	A
1 - 2 ½" x 21" strip, subcut into:	
4 - 4 ½" squares	B
1 - 1 ½" x 21" strip, subcut into:	
8 - 1 ½" squares	C

Block - Fat Eighth	
1 - 5 ¼" x 21" strip, subcut into:	
2 - 5 ¼" squares	D

Block - 10" square	
From the 10" square cut:	
1 - 5 ¼" square	E

Block - Eight 10" squares	
From each 10" square cut:	
1 - 1 ½" square	F

Piecing Instructions:

Cut the Fabric A square, Fabric D squares and Fabric E square on the diagonal twice.

Make four.

Make eight.

Make four.

Assemble Unit. Press open.

Hourglass Unit should measure 4 ½" x 4 ½".

Make four.

ssemble Unit.

enter Unit should measure 4 ½" x 4 ½".

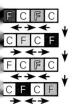

ake one.

ssemble Block. Press open.

immer Block should measure 12 ½" x 12 ½".

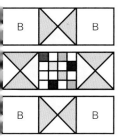 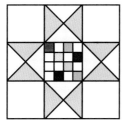

ake one.

Sunshine Block

12 ½" x 12 ½"
Make one

Cutting Instructions:

Background - Fat Quarter		
4 - 2 ½" x 21" strips, subcut into:		
4 - 2 ½" x 4 ½" rectangles		A
4 - 2 ½" squares		B
16 - 2 ½" squares		C

Block - 10" square		
From the 10" square cut:		
1 - 4 ½" square		D

Block - 10" square		
From the 10" square cut:		
4 - 2 ½" x 4 ½" rectangles		E

Block - Fat Eighth		
2 - 2 ½" x 21" strips, subcut into:		
4 - 2 ½" x 4 ½" rectangles		F
4 - 2 ½" squares		G

Piecing Instructions:

Draw a diagonal line on the wrong side of the Fabric C squares.

With right sides facing, layer a Fabric C square on one end of a Fabric F rectangle.

Stitch on the drawn line and trim ¼" away from the seam.

Repeat on the opposite end.

Outer Flying Geese Unit should measure 2 ½" x 4 ½".

Make four.

With right sides facing, layer a Fabric C square on one end of a Fabric E rectangle.

Stitch on the drawn line and trim ¼" away from the seam.

Repeat on the opposite end.

Inner Flying Geese Unit should measure 2 ½" x 4 ½".

Make four.

ssemble Unit.

ying Geese Unit should measure 4 ½" x 4 ½".

ake four.

ssemble Unit.

uter Unit should measure 4 ½" x 4 ½".

ake four.

Assemble Block. Press open.

Sunshine Block should measure 12 ½" x 12 ½".

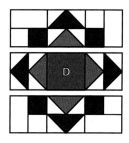 

Make one.

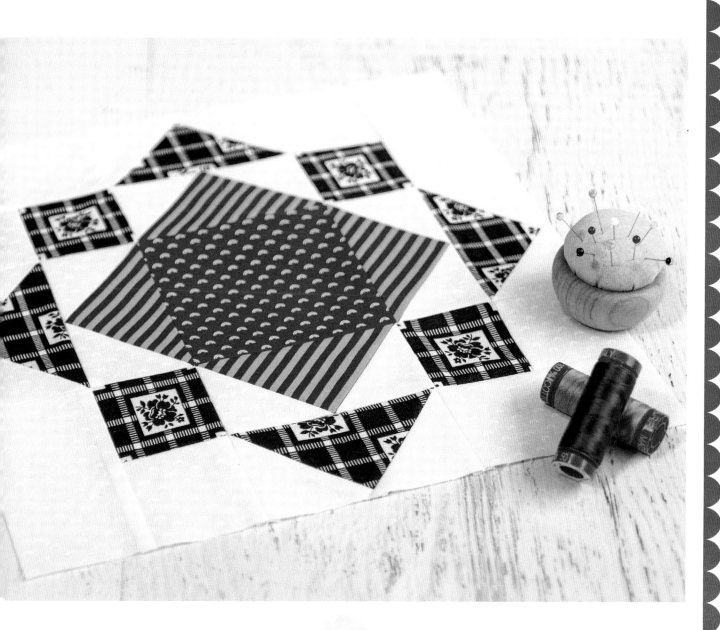

Shine On Sampler Finishing

Cutting Instructions:

Background & Borders - 1 ¼ yards	
4 - 2 ½" x WOF strips, subcut into:	
2 - 2 ½" x 8 ½" rectangles	A
1 - 2 ½" x 6 ½" rectangle	B
1 - 2 ½" x 4 ½" rectangle	C
38 - 2 ½" squares	D
8 - 2 ½" x WOF strips, sew end to end and subcut into:	
2 - 2 ½" x 76 ½" strips	E
2 - 2 ½" x 68 ½" strips	F
2 - 1 ¾" x WOF strips, subcut into:	
2 - 1 ¾" x 30 ½" strips	G
2 - 1 ½" x WOF strips, subcut into:	
2 - 1 ½" x 14 ½" rectangles	H
2 - 1 ½" x 6 ½" rectangles	I

Blocks - Five 10" squares

From each 10" square cut:	
1 - 2 ½" square	J

Blocks - 10" square

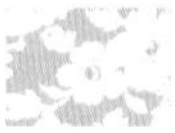

From the 10" square cut:	
3 - 2 ½" x 4 ½" rectangles	K

Blocks - 10" square

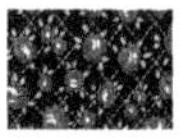

From the 10" square cut:	
3 - 2 ½" x 4 ½" rectangles	L

Blocks - Thirteen 10" squares

From each 10" square cut:	
1 - 2 ½" x 4 ½" rectangle	M

Binding - ⅞ yard

| 9 - 2 ½" x WOF strips | N |

Backing - 5 ⅛ yards

Quilt Center:

Draw a diagonal line on the wrong side of the Fabric D squares.

With right sides facing, layer a Fabric D square on the top end of a Fabric M rectangle.

Stitch on the drawn line and trim ¼" away from the seam.

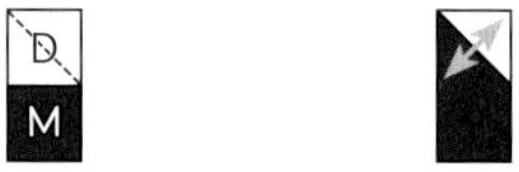

Repeat on the bottom end.

Scrappy Flying Geese Unit should measure 2 ½" x 4 ½".

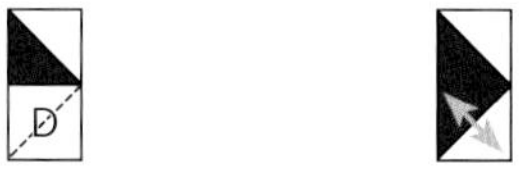

Make one from each 10" square.
Make thirteen total.

Assemble Block. Press open.
Six Scrappy Flying Geese Block should measure 4 ½" x 12 ½".

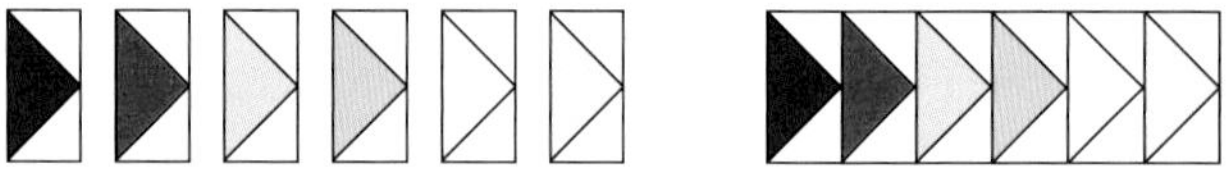

Make one.

Assemble Unit. Press open.
Section One Unit should measure 12 ½" x 16 ½".

Make one.

semble Block. Press open.

rdered Beehive Block should measure 8 ½" x 12 ½".

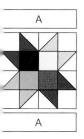

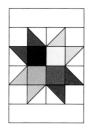

ake one.

semble Block. Press open.

ction One Block should measure 34 ½" x 44 ½".

ake one.

th right sides facing, layer a Fabric D square on one end of a Fabric K rectangle.

itch on the drawn line and trim ¼" away from the seam.

peat on the opposite end.

een Flying Geese Unit should measure 2 ½" x 4 ½".

ke three.

Shine On Sampler Finishing

With right sides facing, layer a Fabric D square on one end of a Fabric L rectangle.

Stitch on the drawn line and trim ¼" away from the seam.

Repeat on the opposite end.

Navy Flying Geese Unit should measure 2 ½" x 4 ½".

Make three.

Assemble Block.

Green and Navy Flying Geese Block should measure 4 ½" x 14 ½".

Make one.

Assemble Unit.

Section Two Unit should measure 10 ½" x 20 ½".

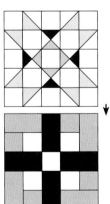   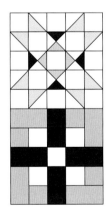

Make one.

Assemble Block.

Section Two Block should measure 20 ½" x 34 ½".

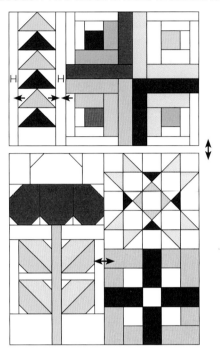

Make one.

Assemble Block.

Seven Scrappy Flying Geese Block should measure 4 ½" x 14 ½".

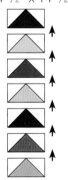   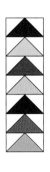

Make one.

ssemble Unit.

ection Three Unit should measure 6 ½" x 12 ½".

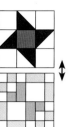

ake one.

ssemble Block.

ection Three Block should measure 30 ½" x 42 ½".

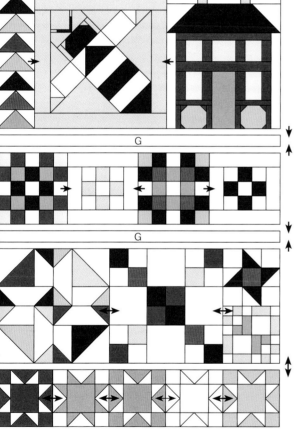

ake one.

Assemble Block. Press open.

Scrappy Five Patch Block should measure
2 ½" x 10 ½".

     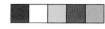

Make one.

Assemble Unit. Press open.

Left Section Four Unit should measure 12 ½" x 18 ½".

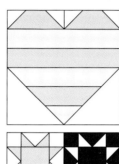   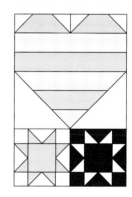

Make one.

Assemble Unit. Press open.

Right Section Four Unit should measure 12 ½" x 18 ½".

Make one.

Shine On Sampler Finishing

Assemble Unit. Press open.

Section Four Unit should measure 18 ½" x 24 ½".

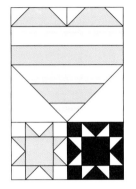  

Make one.

Assemble Block. Press open.

Section Four Block should measure 34 ½" x 42 ½".

Make one.

Quilt Assembly:

ssemble Quilt Center Press open.

uilt Center should measure 64 ½" x 76 ½".

tach side borders using the Fabric E strips.

tach top and bottom borders using the Fabric F strips.

inishing:

ece the Fabric N strips end to end for binding.

uilt and bind as desired.

Shine On Cross Stitch

Designed by Bonnie Olaveson & Camille Roskelley
Stitched by Dana Gonsalves
Sample was stitched on Cloud 25 Count Lugana by Lori Holt for Zweigart using Cosmo Thread

Shine On Cross Stitch

While sewing Weekender blocks late one night at a quilt retreat, my cross stitch loving friend Dana saw a picture of the Shine On Sampler. The first thing she said was "I need to stitch that." I agreed, I needed to stitch it too! It was just the perfect little bonus project and the book wouldn't be complete without it. We got to work on a cross stitch version of the quilt as soon as I returned home and Dana, my mom and I starting stitching. Since it was her idea, it only felt right that Dana stitch the sample for the book, and she did a beautiful job. Cross stitching is such a relaxing way to unwind at the end of a long day, and whether you stitch just one block or the whole sampler, this project is surely one that you'll cherish.

— *Camille*

Shine On Cross Stitch

Cross Stitch Information:

Stitch Count 153w x 190h

Fabric Count	Finished Size	Suggested Fabric Size
14 count Aida	11" x 13.5"	17" x 20"
25 count Lugana	12.25" x 15.25"	18" x 21"
28 count Linen	11" x 13.5"	17" x 20"

		Cosmo	DMC	Skeins
Red		800	666	3
Dark Pink		834	3706	1
Light Pink		851	3713	1
Nectarine		2402	3854	1
Sunshine		2297	727	1
Light Green		324	907	1
Dark Green		325A	470	1
Light Aqua		896	964	2
Dark Aqua		897	959	3
Navy		168	336	2
White		100	Blanc	1

2 strands of DMC/Cosmo

General Cross Stitch Instructions:

Since many of you are quilters who may be new to cross stitch, or just dusting off your cross stitch supplies, we thought it might be helpful to include a few cross stitch basics to get you started.

You'll need to gather your cloth of choice, floss, size 26 tapestry needle and a hoop that measures at least 6" around. A needle minder is also very helpful to keep track of your needle.

Cut an 18" piece of floss and use two strands to start stitching. Trim your cloth to the suggested fabric size. Start in the top left corner of the diagram leaving 3" of extra cloth all the way around. Work on one block at a time and move from left to right. Note that if you use Lugana or Linen, you stitch over two threads.

How to cross stitch:

1. To begin stitching, bring the threaded needle up from the back of the fabric leaving about a 1" tail of thread at the back.
2. Stitch the next five to six stitches over the tail of thread to secure.
3. Pass your threaded needle through a hole diagonally across from where you started.
4. Continue stitching following the diagram to complete a row of half stitches.
5. Complete the row of stitches going the other direction. It is important that all the X's are crossed in the same direction.
6. Keep stitching until you near the end of the thread.
7. On the back side of the fabric, pass the needle through at least three completed stitches to secure the thread.

14 count Aida

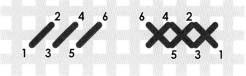

25 count Lugana/Linen

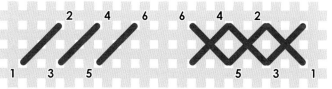

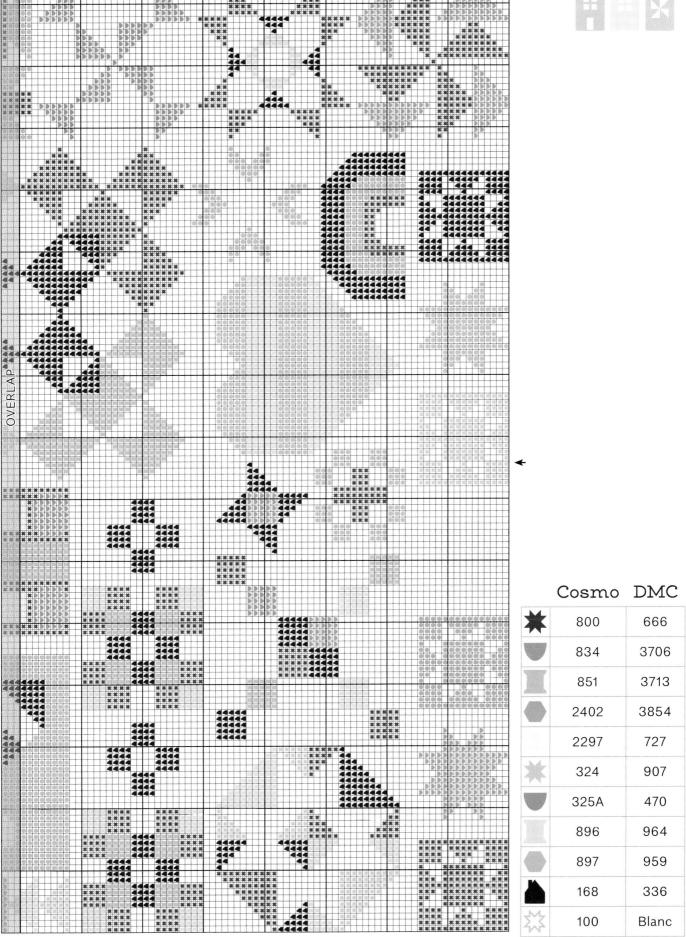

	Cosmo	DMC
✴	800	666
◖	834	3706
⬛	851	3713
⬡	2402	3854
	2297	727
✳	324	907
◖	325A	470
⬛	896	964
⬡	897	959
⬛	168	336
✶	100	Blanc

The Basics

Every quilter does things a little bit differently, and there is no wrong way to sew as long as you are enjoying it. We thought it might be helpful to share a few of our favorite ways of doing things and some additional quilting information.

All of the quilts in this book were made with 100% cotton premium quality quilting fabric. Quilting cotton is usually considered to be 44-45" wide, but because it usually isn't quite that, we assume 42" to be safe. In this book, WOF is defined as width of fabric throughout.

Some of the collections featured in this book may be out of print, but similar Bonnie & Camille fabrics can be found in your favorite online or local quilt shops.

Tools you'll need:

To make the quilts in this book, you'll need a few basic tools. A sewing machine and ¼" presser foot, rotary cutte ruler that measures at least 2" x 12" and a cutting mat at least 12" x 24". Larger mats and rulers can make cuttir yardage easier. Sewing machine needles, thread and pins are also needed.

The ¼" seam:

The most important quilting skill just might be a good ¼" seam. Using your sewing machine and ¼" presser foot sew two test pieces of fabric together, taking care to line up the edge of the fabric with the edge of the presser foot. When you finish, measure the seam and make any adjustments needed until the seam measures ¼".

Batting and thread:

We use 100% cotton batting and thread for all of our quilting projects. Warm and White is our favorite batting, ar Aurifil 50wt thread is our very favorite thread to sew with.

Pinning and pressing:

As a general rule, pinning at each intersection or every 3" while piecing is a good rule of thumb. We use fine glass head pins and have found they work really well for even the smallest piecing. Pressing is an important step in quilting and can drastically affect your results. Typically we press toward the dark side, but more importantly, we press alternating directions so our seams can nest. When pressing, lift the iron and place it on the area you'd like to flatten. Don't slide it around, just lift it and move it to the next piece. Handle your fabric carefully so it doesn' distort when pressing. In this book, press seams as arrows indicate throughout.

Background fabric:

We use many different background fabrics in our quilting, but a few of our favorites are Moda Bella Solid in Off White (SKU# 9900-200), Moda Cross Weave in Black (SKU# 12119-53) and the white on white fabrics that we include in each of our collections.

A note on pre-washing:

Although many quilters do pre-wash their fabric, we prefer to complete the quilt and then wash it. We typically wash our quilts on a gentle cycle in a non high efficiency washing machine. We use cold water with mild deterge and a few Shout color catchers, then dry in the dryer on gentle. This is our favorite method, but of course, there are many different ways to launder quilts, and you should find the way that works best for you.

A Precut Primer

er the years, we have designed many fabric collections with Moda Fabrics, and all of the quilts in this book use ose fabrics in various ways. Our fabric collections typically include 40 coordinating fabrics that are released ice a year. Using precut fabrics is a wonderful and simple way to make a beautiful quilt but can be a little tricky keep straight. Here's a bit more info on our favorite fabric treats.

at Quarters and Fat Eighths:

t quarters are very versatile cuts of fabric that can be used for just about erything. They measure 18" x 21", are easy to collect and are the perfect way build a fabric stash. A fat quarter bundle typically includes one fat quarter m each print in a fabric collection, all tied up in a pretty bow. Fat eighths are nilar to fat quarters, only half the size. They measure 9" x 21" and also come in ndles.

Jelly Rolls and Honey Buns:

Possibly the cutest of the precuts, Jelly Rolls include 40 - 2 ½" x 44" strips cut from a collection of fabric rolled up into a cute little roll. Honey Buns are similar to Jelly Rolls, only instead of being 2 ½" wide, the 40 strips are cut 1 ½" wide. These precut strips can be used for many different quilts and are definitely time savers.

ayer Cakes, Charm Packs and Mini Charm Packs:

ese precuts definitely come in handy for a variety of projects and come in ree different sizes. Layer Cakes include 42 - 10" squares from one fabric llection. Charm Packs include 42 - 5" squares from one fabric collection, and ni Charm Packs include 42 - 2 ½" squares from one fabric collection.

Scraps:

Quilters are well known for keeping every last scrap of fabric to use later on, and we are certainly guilty of this! We save all of our little fabric bits and precut pieces and add them to our scrap bins as we sew. In fact, many of the quilts made in this book were made entirely from favorite scraps we've saved over the years. A word of advice? Save those scraps!

Quilting Your Quilt

There are many options when it comes to finishing a quilt. Hand quilting, quilting on your domestic machine and having a quilt longarmed are just a few of the options we have used. For larger quilts in particular, a longarm quilter is especially helpful. We asked our favorite longarm quilters for some tips on sending your quilts to have them quilted and here were their suggestions.

Abby Latimer, Latimer Lane Quilting
(Instagram: @latimerlanequilts)

· Choosing a quilting design can be a little nerve-wracking, even for a longarm quilter. When I choose a design for a customer quilt or one of my own quilts, I pay attention to scale and busy-ness of the overall quilt and fabric. Sometimes a busy quilt needs a simple design and vice versa. The quilting pattern needs to complement or balance the quilt top, and with practice, choosing a quilting design does get easier with time.

· My personal preference is to choose a thread color that is lighter rather than darker and blends well with the background color. More and more people are asking for quilts to be quilted in white. It gives the quilt wonderful texture without becoming the focal point of the quilt. I never want the quilting to take away from the piecing. The quilt blocks should be the focal point, not the quilting. It should complement all of your hard work, not hide it!

Susan Hansen, SuzyQ's Quilting
(Instagram: @suzyq2k1)

· Take the time to square your blocks. This step is key to having the desired result when everything is finished a lays flat and square.

· Trim your threads on the back, especially if you have a white top as they may show through.

· Press your quilt top. Examine it and make sure all is well. It's easier to fix anything that might not be quite flat straight at this stage than after it is quilted.

Nicole Christoffersen, Kwilt It Longarm Quilting
(Instagram: @kwilter100)

· One thing I would suggest is to piece the backing fabric horizontally whenever possible. It helps the backing li flat, so you avoid fabric bulk or puckering in the back.

· Make sure your backing is at least 6-8" bigger than your quilt top, and double check with your longarm quilter for what they prefer. A back that is too small can really impact the overall quilting on the quilt!

· I would also make sure you communicate with your longarm quilter. They get to know your style over time and can help you choose designs based on your style. So, if you love a design on a quilt, let them know! If you are crazy about how a design looks on a quilt, let them know. The same goes with density of designs. That way th can get to know your personal preferences better and customize their service to you.

Binding Your Quilt

Camille's Machine Binding Technique:

Sew your 2 ½" binding strips end to end and press in half lengthwise.

Sew to the back of your quilt, connecting ends right sides together. Pull the binding around to the front of the quilt and clip in place.

Stitch the binding down just inside the binding edge. A regular ¼" foot will do.

When you reach a corner, stop a few inches from the corner, miter, secure with a pin and continue stitching.

Bonnie's Hand Binding Technique:

Sew your 2 ½" binding strips end to end and press in half lengthwise.

Stitch the binding to the front of the quilt using a ¼" seam.

When you get to a corner, stop ¼" before the corner, backstitch, remove quilt from under the presser foot.

Fold binding upward making sure the quilt top and binding form a straight line.

Holding the fold in place, bring the binding down in line with the quilt edge, continue stitching binding.

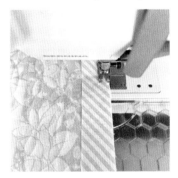

When binding is machine stitched on, bring folded edge around to back of quilt, hand stitch in place, mitering corners.

Shine On by Bonnie & Camille ©

About
Bonnie & Camille

Bonnie and Camille met on June 10, 1983, when Camille came into the world on Bonnie's 24th birthday. Not only do the two share a family and a birthday, they also share a love of quilting and an all-out obsession with fabric.

Since starting her company Cotton Way in 1990, Bonnie has designed over 300 patterns. She currently resides in Idaho, has a wonderful husband, five children and enjoys spoiling her 20 beautiful grandchildren. When she's not busy designing, she enjoys decorating her home and boating with the family.

Camille's pattern company Thimble Blossoms published its first pattern in 2007, and she has since designed over 150 patterns, written two books and has taught many classes both online and in person. A few of her favorite things are sewing with friends, spending time at the lake with her family and cookies of any kind. She has three boys that keep her busy.

This mother-daughter duo has designed over 20 fabric collections with Moda Fabrics throughout the years and both love a good sewing day together.

Connect with us:

Bonnie -
www.cottonway.com
Instagram @bonniecottonway

Camille -
www.thimbleblossoms.com
Instagram @thimbleblossoms

Our Facebook group: facebook.com/groups/bcquiltcrew